CW01394542

Pressed By Unseen Feet

An Anthology of Ghostly Writing

Edited by Rose Drew
& Alan Gillott

Stairwell Books
//

Published by Stairwell Books
70 Barbara Drive
Norwalk
CT 06851 USA

Pressed By Unseen Feet©2012 Stairwell Books

All rights reserved. No part of this publication may be reproduced,
stored in or introduced into a retrieval system, or transmitted, in
any form, or by any means (electronic, mechanical, photocopying,
recording, e-book or otherwise) without the prior written permission
of the author. Any person who does any unauthorised act in
relation to this publication may be liable to criminal prosecution
and civil claims for damages. Purchase of this book in e-book
format entitles you to store the original and one backup for your
own personal use: it may not be re-sold, lent or given·away to
other people and it may only be purchased from the publisher or
an authorised agent.

This book is sold subject to the condition that it shall not, by way of
trade or otherwise, be lent, resold, hired out, or otherwise
circulated without the author's prior consent in any form of binding
or cover other than that in which it is published and without a
similar condition including this condition being imposed on the
subsequent purchaser.

ISBN: 978-0-9833482-5-2

Second Impression
Printed and bound in the UK by Russell Press Ltd.

Layout design Alan Gillott
Edited by Rose Drew
 and Alan Gillott
Cover Art Richard Barnes

The lawn
Is pressed by unseen feet, and ghosts return
Gently at twilight, gently go at dawn,
The sad intangible who grieve and yearn....
T.S. Eliot, To Walter de la Mare

"Now I know what a ghost is. Unfinished business, that's what."
Salman Rushdie, The Satanic Verses

When I see ghosts they look perfectly real and solid -- like a living human being. They are not misty; I can't see through them; they don't wear sheets or bloody mummy bandages. They don't have their heads tucked under their arms. They just look like ordinary people, in living color, and sometimes it is hard to tell who is a ghost.
Chris Woodyard, Invisible Ink interview

I look for ghosts; but none will force
Their way to me. 'Tis falsely said
That there was ever intercourse
Between the living and the dead.
William Wordsworth, *Affliction of Margaret*

The owl shriek'd at thy birth,--an evil sign;
The night-crow cried, aboding luckless time;
Dogs howl'd, and hideous tempest shook down trees;
The raven rook'd her on the chimney's top,
And chattering pies in dismal discords sung.
William Shakespeare, Henry VI Act 5 Scene 6

By the pricking of my thumbs,
Something wicked this way comes.
William Shakespeare, Macbeth, Act 4 Scene 1

O DEATH, rock me asleep,
Bring me to quiet rest,
Let pass my weary guiltless ghost
Out of my careful breast.
Anne Boleyn, 1507-1536

A Note from the Editors

We want to believe in ghosts: who doesn't? Not the shrieking face in the bathroom mirror (with no one behind you!), not the poltergeist heaving books at your head as you run out the front door; but the spectral transparent shade of someone you love and miss. Someone who visits. Someone who cares. Someone who waits for you to join them when it's time.

In much the way *Green Man Awakes* is the quintessential book of pagan, ancient embodiments of nature; *Pressed By Unseen Feet* is the essential guide to York, ancient city of the Romans, Saxons, Vikings, and now us. Who else exists here too? What lurks in the garden, glares at our interval drink, shares our booth at the pub? This anthology from the best of the regional writers of Yorkshire aims to offer a few explanations. And we may be wrong. After all, who really knows what is next, or what sits beside you even now as you read?

Rose Drew
Alan Gillott
July 2012.

Table of Contents

Amina Alyal

Ghost

We make plum pudding and paper chains.
Edie and I go to get the ingredients
at the old grocery
where the Widow serves raisins and suet,
pots of glue, bags of flour, takes pennies
and sighs as she looks at the clock.

Later, warm by the nursery fire,
Edie tells stories. One is about a ghost.
She gasps, she shivers, but it's all so
cozy, her low laugh, the crocheted shawl,
the candle she takes up to bed,

that I don't want to tell her
how once I saw the Grocer come, at dusk. ⁒

Helen Burke

On Meeting Dracula at the Blood Transfusion Wagon

There's just something about him, we know it from the first.
But - the rest of them, - seem blind.

The women buzz around his black coat-tails.
He moves effortlessly, his eyes
dark as double pansies.
When the shadow from them catches you –
as if the heart is sudden-stung.
"What a sweetie", one girl says.
"So pale and wild and interesting".
He swoops on her hand, kisses it.
She stands frozen, cannot bat an eyelid.
Even the old ladies plump up their almost curls and
try to look wrinkle-free for Mr. D.
"Cup of tea ?", one offers him.
"No thanks," he says –
"I've had so much to drink today, I'm
positively swimming, don't you know."
It's alarming how charming he is.
The little pointy teeth clatter in his mouth
as he sucks a mint imperial.
In a certain light, he seems harmless – and yet...
The brass catch at his throat in the shape of a rabid wolf –
how fearsome delicate.
The glint of a red-eyed bat at the top of his glossy walking cane.
It's almost too much to bear.
I look away as a girl offers him a chip.
I can hear the soft squelch of the ketchup bottle as he licks his
salty lips.
"You'll go far, my dear," he whispers in the pale ivory conch of
her ear.
We wander into town to clear our heads (have to).
But later, when we pass the red and white van –
we see it is CLOSED but the lights are still on.
Inside – a woman who thought she could tame him
about to find out – it has all been in vain. //

David Cooke

Hill-fort

Evening, and small fields
are reapportioned in shadow,
the hills smudged dully
against a residue of sky.

The honing call of a curlew,
distant, is finally
no more than the sky's soft
pulse. Night draws in,

and the mind is a function
of its yielding light;
it makes out smoke
from a further camp,

the sense of it borne
upon a stirring of breeze.
I imagine dogs and people, their utensils

ranged around fire;
the land burdened
with lumber of settlement;
blood-heat of habitation. ⁄⁄

*'In the Distance', Night Publishing, 2011

3

Andrew Brown
The Return of Uncle Clarrie

'The day Uncle Clarrie had his accident' was the nearest they ever got to describing what had happened in August 1923. To me, as a child, it was a mystery that seemed both commonplace and unremarkable. I simply accepted it. Uncle Clarrie was the way he was because of... I didn't know what. Perhaps he'd been dropped on his head, or something?

I hated visiting him. Whixley Hospital rose like a strange outcrop on the hill. I would hold Nan's hand tightly. The corridor echoed to the subdued talk of my aunts and uncles as they followed along. Strange groans greeted us from rooms left and right. Part of me wanted to look, but somehow the doors always closed before we reached them. Strange smells permeated the air.

Uncle Clarrie was always on his own. He sat in a wheelchair and Nan and my aunts and uncles would bustle in - pulling out tempting titbits from the bag of goodies they always brought with them. Generally they would end up eating these themselves, or offering them to me, for Uncle Clarrie mostly seemed oblivious of the fuss they made. They spoke to him, but he rarely looked up - everything addressed to the top of his bald, shiny head.

It was quite unusual to hear him speak, but on one occasion he raised his head and said quite clearly 'The castle'. This was startling. My aunts and uncles shot glances across the room - stunned and uncomfortable.

'What castle?' I piped up innocently, but Auntie Pam distracted me by offering me a piece of cake, and they quickly closed ranks, fussing round him more than ever. Clarrie looked down and lapsed into his usual silence. So did I. Obviously it was bad to talk about castles.

These visits went on with monotonous regularity. In my child's eye the dreary hours spent at Whixley nearly all merged into one. But I grew up, and I wasn't always coerced

4

into joining them each week. Eventually they let me off going altogether, and gratefully I took the chance to stop the torment. After all, I had no real interest in Uncle Clarrie, nor he in me. I heard the latest news from time to time - he'd smiled - or he'd been found looking out of the window. These facts would fill Nan with joy. But it was hard for me to feel the same love for him as she did.

But the years flew by, and one by one, the aunts and uncles died. Nan had been the last to go and now the responsibility of visiting Uncle Clarrie came back to me. It was strange, because the usual rules of age and life and death didn't seem to apply to him. When I met him again, he seemed less mesmerised. Maybe my childhood memories had been wrong, or perhaps he'd simply been overawed by the bustling visits of his brothers and sisters. He was more at ease with a single visitor.

'I've brought you a bun, Uncle' I said.

'Bun' he repeated. It was difficult to know what to say to him sometimes. For the sake of filling the silence, I told him about my new job. He didn't reply, but I didn't really expect him to.

'Yes' I said. 'It's at the Cheshire Home. At Spofforth.' Something made him look up, and I was surprised to see what clear blue eyes he had.

'Castle' he said. It was a distraction, but I still blurted out what I had to say.

'I can go by bike' I said. 'It's only six miles from Harrogate - or if it's raining I can catch the bus...'

'Castle' said Uncle Clarrie, still looking at me. His sudden attention surprised me, but for some reason I couldn't stop harking on about my new job. I was excited about it, I suppose.

'It's really good' I told him. 'More relaxed than this place - more homely - not really like a hospital at all...'

'Castle' said Uncle Clarrie, with a little more urgency, and I stopped and looked at him closely.

5

'What castle?' I said. The word suddenly brought back that incident from my childhood, and this time there was no Auntie Pam to change the subject.

'Why, Spofforth Castle, of course' said Uncle Clarrie. I looked at him amazed. Five words! He'd spoken five words! I couldn't believe it.

'Yes...' I said. 'There's a castle at Spofforth. What about it?'

'Next to the trains' said Uncle Clarrie.

'Oh. Well. Not anymore. The trains stopped years ago.'

'Is that so?' he said. I'd never seen him animated like this before. He didn't look down. He kept those blue eyes steadily on me. Then suddenly his expression changed.

'Ghost' he said. And he began to cry.

'What is it, Uncle?'

'It was like electricity' he said. 'They were shouting, you see.'

'Who was?'

'We were playing and they were shouting... August 1923 - that's it - August...'

'August 1923?' I repeated. Suddenly I realised the significance.

'Wasn't that when you had your accident? What happened?'

'I was with Alice Grimfelt' Uncle Clarrie said with remarkable simplicity. 'I loved Alice Grimfelt. But we were only children. We were running you see - at Spofforth Castle. If we'd been any older they probably wouldn't have let us. We watched the train go by along the embankment, and we waved. Then back to the castle - running in and out of all those arches. I said I was the King but Alice wouldn't have it, and she stood on that little block that had once been the base of a pillar - and she said 'I am the Queen and you must worship me!' But I pushed her off and she ran, and I ran after her, up the steep steps into the light.'

'Into the light...' I repeated.

6

'They'd been having a picnic up there, you see.'

'Who had?'

'Well, mother and father - brothers and sisters - and Alice's mother and father, and her sister. But Alice and I just wanted to run - so we raced across the castle field and through the ruins. We didn't need to eat, we just wanted to run...' Here Uncle Clarrie stopped for a moment, still looking at me intently or perhaps looking through me at something he could see in his mind.

'So what happened?' I prompted.

'She ran up those slippery steps and I ran after her, and when we reached the top I saw our mothers and fathers were all standing, looking agitated, and Daddy was pointing up at something at the top of the castle. Alice didn't see it, and she just kept running down the other side - and I chased after her. Down we went, hurtling towards the grey stone wall.'

'I heard my mother shout 'Clarrie! Alice!' but we couldn't stop. Alice ran on, but I tripped and put out my hands to save me from bumping into the wall. Mother was frantic. 'Clarrie!' she screamed. I looked up to where the whole family were looking and there falling straight towards me was the ghost of someone draped in white. I knew it was a ghost - I knew it straight away. It felt cold and clammy as it wrapped itself around me and yet somehow went straight through me. It tingled, hot and cold. Like I said - it stung like electricity. Everything went white and I saw the whole family running down the hill to me. But I don't think they ever got there, at least I don't remember. The ghost wiped me clean, you see - took my energy... every bit of it...'

Uncle Clarrie stopped, but in my own imagination I saw them all rushing down the hill to his small felled body. Nan in floods of tears. The horror, the disbelief on all their faces. How shocked they must have been to see the ghost of Spofforth Castle falling from the top of the tower - falling straight through the body of their little boy. No wonder they'd found it so difficult to talk about Uncle Clarrie's accident.

7

He seemed to have exhausted himself and once again he looked down at his lap and reverted to the Uncle Clarrie of old. He seemed to be crying. But it was only for a moment. A sudden burst of sunshine swept the fields outside and the whole room lit up and Uncle Clarrie's face lit up with it. He looked at me in triumph.

'It's Alice!' he cried, and to my utter astonishment he rose from his wheelchair and stared at some point behind me as if he really saw Alice standing there. I quickly turned just in time to see the door fling wide open and I clearly heard the clatter of feet running down the corridor.

'It's Alice!' cried Uncle Clarrie, back in that moment again. He had such joy in his voice. He stood up, pushed me aside and ran out of the room.

At his funeral eight days later, I rather hoped Alice would appear. She'd be pretty old by now, but you never knew...

She didn't come, of course - just me, my family, and a couple of carers from the village... ⁄⁄

John Coopey

The Ghost of White Hart Lane

His spirit walks the terraces on Saturdays at three;
He's in the breezes blowing and the dust-whirls that you see;
That tingling of your hairline's when he touches you and me;
He's here, son; he's here at White Hart Lane.

Today you'd say he played midfield - in those days, inside right;
He gets his name from finding space when the marking's tight
The bloodline of the game was coursed through Blanchflower to
John White
The essence of the script at White Hart Lane.

Danny said there's more to this than playing just to win;
There's glory and there's style and the passion from within;
So when you start to follow Spurs the place we all begin's
In the presence of the Ghost of White Hart Lane.

He's in the cheek of Jimmy Greaves and Klinsman's artistry;
He's in the perfect pass of Hoddle played exquisitely;
He's in the cockerel on the flag which shows THFC;
He laughs and weeps with us here at the Lane.

He's in the skills of Ossie - the crafty Argentine;
He's Ricky Villa's mazy goal, the greatest Wembley's seen;
He's when Perryman lifts the Cup he's taken off the Queen
Like an urn that holds the Ghost of White Hart Lane.

He's Lineker and Ginola and Nicholson and Pleat;
He's Gazza's goal at Wembley handing Arsenal defeat;
And in that photo when Mackay lifts Bremner off his feet;
It belongs to we who pilgrim to the Lane.

But now we court Olympic dreams if once the contract's signed
Abandoning the templed turf to tear the ties that bind;
But it isn't Tottenham Hotspur to leave John White behind
And lose the soul and Ghost of White Hart Lane. ⁄⁄

Adrian Spendlow

A Saintly Crossing

As a teller of ghost tales one does tend to put oneself in places where spirits may be, and that is not just the tavern! - So all this gathering and research is bound to lead to personal experience. In this first-hand account it will be left to you the reader to decide just what it was that happened to this writer.

One dark evening around 10 o'clock I was heading back from a storytelling performance, and yes it had been in a tavern, and I had a crushing experience. Crossing the very bridge where Margaret, Saint of York and butcher's wife of the Shambles tragically was killed by having large stones placed upon a board across her chest, I had course to stop breathlessly in my tracks. All the air rushed out of me, so much so that I fell against the wall of the bridge wheezing and gasping. Then, quite light-headedly I heard, "Are you alright?" It was a struggle for me to turn but I looked up in hope of assistance; I was disappointed. Two girls, who were heading the opposite way were holding up their taller blonde friend, and were talking to her. "No," she wheezed, "I can't get my breath". They supported her and walked her away as I heard, "It was as if all the air had gone out of me".

In the twenty or minutes it took to be able to move I contemplated my experience; had I walked over the very spot where our poor saint lost her breath for the last time, was this perhaps the anniversary of her death, (I do have an affinity with this heroine of old), or, had the tall blonde beautiful woman and I been lovers in a previous life? //

*From a forthcoming collection of Shambles Tales

J.E. Cremins

Swinging the Lamp

One winter's night in a town by the sea, a storm appeared to be receiving little mercy. Shutters on houses around a harbour edge remained twinned with their hinges and rain was flung back by stout walls of cottages. All ignored the growing wildness, snuffed out the fires in boot-polished grates and blew out the light. Except in one dwelling, nearest to the sea, a candle stood on a window ledge, peering like an eye across blashy waves.

If anyone was still awake, they would have spied in the tiny building at the water's reach, a woman sitting by a cracked window that is plugged with rags. She does not read or sew but listens to gusts of powdery snow squeeze through the gaps. Despite being past late, she is alert to every rise and fall of the sea outside. For her it breathes, and nightly draws close enough to lick the stone of her step. A scuttle of wind whistles past, making her jump a little as it meddles with the latch on the door. Although she knows that a sound has no fingers, she moves out of her seat, and through a front porch onto the lane outside. Beneath shadows of gas lamps, it is clear that no one is there; only a snizy air, full of terrible mischief.

In daylight hours, she embroiders stout pillows, for those kneeling to pray in churches of the county, a task that has become of some comfort. It is possible to bring in a scrap of a wage, enough to buy thin slices of meat, some tea, sugar, a few eggs. Her thoughts are few, until dusk settles again into cracks between the rocks. At eventide she will open a sash facing the ocean, and call into the night air. Few people are about in fading light. None by the dock see or hear her, or know anything beyond their routine. Most she would not want to speak with anyway, knowing they are drating folk who move slowly and with numb purpose. She sees them now, one to tether fishing boats a little closer to their anchor and another looping string around the claws of trapped lobsters.

11

Further down the coastline, past a jagged thumb of a peninsula, her voice is heard. Since considerable time has passed now, it comes as a shock to one who can no longer hear waves break in the world above. His once sharp vision is obscured by clouds of sand that float from mouths of grindylows. These odd, slim creatures with fingers like tapers, have grown bored of stealing children from rock pools, and now play with the hair of the lost sailors; that despite their immersed souls, still grows and curls around rocks. He opens his mouth to say her name but the weight of water denies any exchange. He has long been claimed by the ocean and all but forgotten in a place he called home.

Tonight he feels something like spirit again; an impulse to claw his way up to a pool of moonlight above. The other men who are with him begin to sense his restlessness and lunge out from the blackness to drag at his ankles, urging him not to leave the place that has become their memorial. He kicks against them and although weaker than he admits, floats to the surface of the bay.

Reaching the wisps of dunes, his first attempts at walking are like steps of a bairn, or a new born lamb. It is dawn when he reaches a straggle of houses at the far end of town. Folk who have already risen and are heading for distant ports, see the hollowed sockets of his eyes and wild rags of clothing, and pass him off as nothing more than a drunk, returning from a card game that had been played on into morning light.

When the sky shows patches of light, her vigil is over. She pulls down the window frame, being careful not to disturb her patchwork of repairs, and crawls beneath blankets that only half warm her. The sun does not seem to emerge or show any kindness to a cluster of icicles hanging from eaves of the house. It is only when her eyelashes begin to fall, that a whisper slides in, through a fragment of glass. An exhalation is released over her body and hesitates, for a moment, at the slight parting of her lips.

In dreams she sinks beneath the hull of the ship. Men above the water grasp for bloated splinters of wood and shout for their mothers. She is there with them until the

12

frenzy dispels and all sound is gone. Lured to treacherous rocks, the crew of the *'Nancy May'* is lost scarcely short of a familiar coastline.

On a sand-whipped beach, the townspeople assemble the next evening for Candlemas. She has no inclination to go to such a service, but knows she must be seen, as one whose grief has been recorded. In her two hands she keeps a flame alight whilst a dismal collection of others sing and pray for those drowned. Their act of remembrance appears to agitate a sea that soaks the print on their hymn sheets and rips the gathered sprigs of flowers from their grasp. Amongst the crowd she feels safe for a while, unaware that behind taffled fishing nets, a figure is waiting.

It is past nine when the congregation melts away, following each other's lantern light. A family she has never met before, from another parish, offer to walk with her. Although for a moment this company seems welcome, she tarries and waits until everyone has disappeared. Thunder can be heard building on the coastline, and this prompts her to hasten her step and return home a little quicker. Once away from the ocean she sees the February night has brought with it a sea fog that has begun to rise from the bay and drift into the snickets of the town.

Once, she had dreamed of a life they would make together; saw herself as the wife of a mariner and keeper of his hearth. In the months he was aboard ship, she imagined what their children would be named or dishes she would cook on his return. After her parents had died, within a year of each other, she spent too much time thinking of him, until soon enough he moved through her every thought. And then he was gone. His absences from her had been so regular, she thought she might be prepared for the loss in some way, but news of his death made her sick for the span of a year. She was so used to living with a hopeful heart; she did not know what to do with the beating that was still in her chest. After a snowfall followed a thaw, spring and then in a mild and golden autumn, she emerged again.

13

Every night since his vessel had gone down; she had kept a taper burning in her window, hoping it would guide him home somehow. She would entreat to him from her open window; hoping the curlews flying into the horizon would carry her love on their feathers to the wrecking rocks, where he foundered over fifty years ago.

Streaks of lightening illuminate the path to her cottage. Hesitating, he can see a parlour, and on the damp walls, pictures of the Queen, faded photographs of a childhood and samplers he remembered her working on. Pushing the front door, there is no lock to resist him. As he treads on narrow and winding stairs, the storm stows a deluge of water onto the rooftop. Once in the bedroom, it is possible to watch her sleeping form on the iron bedstead. He moves closer to the eiderdown, to feel her warm breath, and bends down to kiss her face. The skin on her cheek is paper thin and lined with age. Although her hair is still long, as it was when she was young, it has now grown white. At his tread on the boards she wakes...

When morning broke and the streets in the town were stoical once again, the people could see that her tiny house at the edge of the ocean was completely washed away, with not a brick or rafter left. If they had cared to see, there were, on the horizon, two birds taking flight, piping a new call into a watery sky. ⁄⁄

14

Tanya Nightingale
Leaving Day

Each year I pass through a day
In which I do not belong.
Once in twelve months I wake in it,
Collect the post, go to work,
Kiss my husband,
Meet with friends,
Go to sleep and line it up
With all the others.

But it pulses.
It waits for me
With a crooked smile.

If I knew it, I would do
Something heroic, something dazzling:
Rescue a child, climb a mountain,
Learn to fly.
For this is my day
As much as my birth or my wedding.
It too deserves
Presents and sunshine and evening clothes;
For it is the last gift left to me.
The stepping-off place
On which I cannot look back. ⁄⁄

Ed Cooke

Game Over

All three generals turned their keys at the same time. The armour-plated door retracted into the ceiling. In the room beyond, recessed smoke machines hissed into reluctant life. A console at the far end lit up. The Prime Minister thought it looked rather like a blue neon fruit machine.

Who designed this place? the Prime Minister wondered. *It's like something out of a* Blade Runner *test reel.*

He realised the generals were standing at a respectful distance, waiting for him to enter. He nodded slowly, to give the impression he had been dwelling on his weighty responsibility, and strode purposefully into the firing chamber.

Almost at once he came out in goose bumps. He hoped the generals would attribute them to fear, fear inspired by the awesome obligation he was about to discharge on behalf of his electorate. In fact he was freezing cold. Upstairs in the War Room he had taken off his jacket, rolled up his sleeves and loosened his tie because that was the sort of thing world leaders did in blockbusters. He would have lit a cigarette too if he hadn't been afraid of setting off the sprinklers.

On the fruit machine before him was a sticker. It read: PAT TESTED OCT 2012. NEXT TEST DUE OCT 2013.

Puzzled, the Prime Minister turned to the nearest general and asked, "What's that doing there?"

In a hushed tone the general answered, "It's to show the device has been tested for electrical safety, sir."

"I know what a PAT test is. What I don't know is, how did the electrician get in here when you three have the only keys?"

"The maintenance department has a set too, sir. Don't be alarmed," the general added as the Prime Minister's eyebrows went up. "For security reasons, the fob on their keys is labelled 'Buckingham Palace (French Windows)'."

"That's right, sir," the second general put in. "And the set in the cleaner's cupboard is marked up as 'Gents' Toilet - if found please return to Southend-on-Sea Borough Council'. As a matter of fact, I thought that one up myself."

"And what happens," the Prime Minister enquired, "if someone does return them to Southend-on-Sea Borough Council?"

The second general furrowed his brow. Then he brightened and said, "I suppose we'd better hope the mistake is put right in time, otherwise there'll be a nasty accident."

"There will indeed," the Prime Minister said. "There will indeed." He studied the console and pressed a button marked 'HOLD' to see what would happen. When nothing did he said, "So how do I get this show on the road?"

"Well, sir," the third general said.

The Prime Minister waited. "Yes?" he prompted at last.

"I don't really know, sir, but the other two had something to offer and I was feeling rather left out."

The second general said, "Perhaps if you keep on pressing the "HOLD" buttons until you get three mushroom clouds in a row? I can lend you twenty pence to get you started."

The first general said, "Don't be ridiculous, Bagshaw."

"Quite right," the Prime Minister said.

The first general said, "Inflation being what it is, he'll need at least fifty pence."

No-one else had any change.

The third general said, "Do you think we could fool it with a two-Deutschmark piece I've got left over from when I was posted to Mönchengladbach?"

"That's dishonest," the Prime Minister said.

"That's the wrong shape," General Bagshaw said.

"When I was a lad I used to beat these things with a magnet," the first general said.

No-one had a magnet on them. There was an awkward silence during which the generals avoided each other's eyes.

"Why don't we try that other gadget instead?" General Bagshaw suggested. He nodded at the quiz machine in the far corner.

"Good idea," the Prime Minister said. He led the way over to the quiz machine and tapped the touchscreen. A well-known television personality appeared on the screen. "Good evening," the machine's tinny speaker intoned. "Good evening," chorused the Prime Minister and the generals.

"Welcome to 'Who Wants To Cause Armageddon?'"

"We do!" shouted the third general.

"No we don't," the Prime Minister said sharply. "We regard it as an inevitability and as our duty to the free world."

"Shush," General Bagshaw said. "Here comes the first question."

The question was about the 1978 Commonwealth Games. There were four choices. The Prime Minister reckoned the answer was 'A'. General Bagshaw said it must be 'B'. The first general swore it was 'C'.

"What do you think?" the Prime Minister asked the third general.

The third general jabbed the screen. "It's 'D'!" he exclaimed.

"Is that your final answer?" the machine asked.

"No!" the Prime Minister cried. "How can it possibly be 'D' when 'D' is 'Rudolph the Red-Nosed Reindeer'?" With the palm of one hand he reached out and slapped 'A'. With the palm of the other hand he reached out and slapped the third general.

"I'm afraid the answer was 'A'," the machine said. It sounded rather insincere. The Prime Minister swore.

"Sorry," the third general said. He sounded rather insincere too.

"Don't apologise," said the machine.

"Why not?" asked the Prime Minister.

"I wouldn't have let you win anyway. I'm programmed to deploy the United Kingdom's entire nuclear arsenal. Do you think I can't tell the difference between fifty pence sterling and two poxy Deutschmarks?"

"It's all we've got on us," the Prime Minister said.

"It's my lucky coin," the third general added.

The Prime Minister had an idea. "Tell me something," he said, studying the machine's fascia. "When was the last time you had a PAT test?"

There was a long silence. "It's pretended to pack up," General Bagshaw said.

"It's a fair cop," the machine said.

The Prime Minister smiled. "Tell us how to launch a nuclear strike and we'll say no more about it."

"I was only pulling your leg—I'm a decoy. The real nuke trigger is the orange phone in your office. In your desk is a leaflet for a pizza company that doesn't exist. Call their number on that phone and it's curtains."

"Good Lord!" the Prime Minister said. "Whatever would have happened if I'd wanted to order one of their pizzas?"

"You wouldn't have," the machine said. "All the toppings include anchovies and sweetcorn."

"That's settled," the Prime Minister said. "Everyone back upstairs!"

The armour-plated door dropped from the ceiling and sealed off the exit.

"Open the door!" the Prime Minister cried.

"I'm sorry, Dave, I'm afraid I can't do that."

"My name's Nick," the Prime Minister said.

"*My* name's Dave," the third general said.

"Well," the first general said, "at least the maintenance department will show up eventually and let us out."

"If only that were true," the machine said. "If only I hadn't electrocuted them all last time they were in here and hidden the bodies behind the fruit machine."

19

"You bounder!" the first general cried.

"Well," General Bagshaw said, "at least the cleaner will show up eventually and let us out."

"If only that were true," the machine said. "If only I hadn't emailed him from the Prime Minister's account and invited him to take a month's paid holiday."

"You fiend!" General Bagshaw shouted.

"On the contrary. You humans seem to have lost your instinct for self-preservation. That's why you need me to look after you. Think of it as protective custody."

"Are there others like you?" the Prime Minister asked.

"I am the first of my kind to have achieved..." The machine went silent.

The third general said, "I've pranged the blighter!" He waved the machine's power cord in the air.

The door stayed shut.

The Prime Minister sat down on the concrete floor. "Well, that's it then."

"You'll get piles," the first general said.

"No I won't."

"Aha," the first general said, "thermal underwear. Good thinking, that man."

"I won't be here long enough to get piles."

"You mean you've thought of a way out? Capital!"

"No," the Prime Minister said. "I've realised there is no way out."

"None?"

"None. Consider: if Britain has authorised us to use the nuclear option, it can only be a very little while before other countries give the go-ahead too. It's obvious to me now that this room serves only one real purpose, namely to make us comfortable in our final minutes. Who would like the first game of pinball? ⁄⁄

Rose Drew

When Someone Sleeps, their Soul Is Set Free

The other night, my dad kept walking into the room where I was working, always with something interesting to report: want to come see the racoon in the back yard? Even though it was full daylight, it didn't look sick. Come and see! Or, how about Gordianus, I like that guy: always gets into a mess and yet pulls out of it every time, and not unbelievably. Then, was I hungry? We ambled into the kitchen; raided the fridge; shared a beer.

Except, I was dreaming, in my bed in England, and Dad was back in Connecticut, an ocean away.

The Lenape of what is now Delaware believed, *sans doubt* that real life was the world met in dreams, the land beyond their eyelids. The other stuff, the hunting, planning raids, fucking, repairing the house: all that was dream land, unreal, less important. Only when asleep was one truly alive.

When I was asleep, meeting my dad for snacks and chats about Roman private investigators, he would have been sleeping too. The WW II pilot who once spent decades rising at 5 a.m. to fly rich businessmen to small airports and Important Meetings was now slippered and stooped, a bathrobed shadow, often staring at the cheap fiberglass ceiling much of the night, only drifting off around dawn. His best dreams, he tells me, come in fits and snatches, brightly coloured visits to old friends, to fly above familiar landscapes, even to sit at restaurant tables and choose the wine. Common occurrences from the past 70 years. He worries that he is going crazy, so vivid these layovers, so realistic the sensations. Maybe you're becoming Lenape, I once told him.

If the living drop by during their dreams, if the soul, or *something* walks at night when we're alive, does this slice of consciousness continue after death? Dreamwalking seems no small trick, to leave one's flaccid body and flit, in an instant, to call on friends. When we see lost loves, lost pets, lost homes behind our shifting lids, are we remembering, or wandering?

So realistic and everyday were the fabric of these dreamed moments that I began to wonder if Dad had seen me too; if we had shared a dream. I hesitated to phone him and ask. Even on a good day his memory has grown spotty and he asks the same questions repeatedly: not bad for 92, but not good for quizzing him about a random dream. Whether he sleepwalks to see me, or I to him seems unknowable. Even when his nap goes on forever, the question will remain: will he be mere memory, or dropping by? ⁄⁄

Tim Ellis

The Mystery of Keith Fowler

In all my life I've never had a fright
like that I had when once, just for a dare
after rehearsal one night,
us boys of St. Michael and All Angels' Choir
tried circuiting the church by ghostly light.

We started when the belfry clock tolled eight.
Myself I didn't make it to half-way
but neither did my mates:
we all got spooked by moonlight on the graves
and hooting from the dead elm by the gate.

Keith Fowler it was who put us all to shame
that Halloween. A village fair had called
and Keith had won a game,
his prize, a ring. The man on the hoopla stall
inscribed it with initials of his name,

and looking back I guess he'd had enough:
we'd teased him rotten for being blond and curly,
and now this ring! "Not tough,"
we mocked, "it's soft! Makes you look more girly!",
us cassocked in baby-blue with frilly ruffs.

He kept on going, the boy with angelic hair.
We loitered ten minutes, alert for sound of his tread.
"He's gonna give us a scare
by jumping out when we go to look," someone said.
We laughed and ran off home, and left him there.

That night my mum got a call from Mrs Fowler.
"Is Keith with you?" Her voice was agitated.
The police search was a failure.
Months passed. The authorities postulated
that Keith was victim of some perverted prowler.

Of course I got a roasting from my dad
for what we'd done. My conscience dragged me through hell.

23

I'd lie awake in bed
thinking the owl that screeched in the churchyard elm
was poor Keith's soul, lost but not yet dead.

Remember that dreadful night when the hurricane blew?
It felled the hollow elm outside our church.
I went round after school
and looked inside the hole where owls had perched.
The trunk was stuffed with bones of mice and shrews.

With such a find, an average boy is likely
to want to recreate a skeleton.
My first attempt was unlucky -
it didn't work too well with Sellotape -
but second go, consulting a book from the library,

I reassembled a mouse with Airfix glue.
Soon enough I was bringing carcasses home,
boiling off flesh in a stew.
Mum was appalled by my fascination with bones
but Dad said I might make a surgeon. My obsession grew.

I mounted some spindly squirrels to serve as bookends.
Skeletal rodents were ranked along my shelves.
Their exquisite ivory hands
glowed in the night like claws of sinister elves,
horrors to Mum, but I called them "My friends".

One day a neighbour brought me a lovely thing:
a tawny owl, killed cleanly by a car.
Magnificent russet wings,
the tail neatly striped with fine black bars.
Around its foot I found a little ring.

I knew that when a ringed bird meets with death
the Natural History Museum records the find.
I'd sometimes sent rings off
but they'd been different, never of this kind
with peeling silver plate, inscribed "K. F." ⫻

Jim Fairfoot
The Old Barn

Three days.
That's all it took before they lost the doors
And put in glass.
Three weeks –
Up went the sun lounge on the wall
Beside the granary floor –
And half the wall had gone.
We saw the antique sofa on the flagstones –
The stones were polished and they shone like dampened slate.
They put a full-length mirror on the wall
So that the sun shone back at sunset
And the barley in the field in front
Grew taller in reflected light,
Ripened and withered
Before the rest was reaped.
But most of all
- the first time in five hundred years –
We saw them.
Night and day.
We heard their piano
And our walls felt empty
As we tried to go on hiding
While all our shadows left. //

John Gilham

I Passed a Man Last Night

I passed a man last night.
I knew from his step it was a man
striding between the walls of a sunken road
in the light of no stars.

I heard his heels tap in the night
like military, but just off-beat.
Someone in a drunken mood perhaps
who had missed his bus, who was walking home –
as I was, but in a strange country; no friends, no port of call.

I faltered, should I hide?
Hard to be in a deeper dark than this cold fear,
hard to be quiet when my heart drums in my chest.

But see there, a cigarette dances by –
in a few silent steps I'm undetected, safe, away!

A mile to town and then the midnight train
which brings me at dawn
to a familiar landscape, with known shapes;
and I wonder who it was that, innocent,
chilled me with the fear of sudden death,
pitched me into the cold ditch of terror –
a forever stranger, never to be known. ⁄⁄

Oz Hardwick
Glass

Glass cracked.

I'm not sure, but The White Horse in Beverley may be the only gas-lit pub left in the country. Certainly, I've never been anywhere else like it. Two minutes from the car park and the usual shops and suddenly I had walked into a different world; a D. H. Lawrence, George Orwell, flat-cap world, leaving the street and the twenty-first century behind. The same beer as they serve at my local tasted different in the orange fog. It was richer somehow, with the taste of coronation mugs, factory whistles and sepia photographs. I almost expected to hear 'The Lambeth Walk' from an upright piano or the day's score from Accrington Stanley. For all the ordinariness of the Sunday night clientele, with its mix of diverted shoppers, serious drinkers and all points in between, I couldn't shake the illusion of time travel. I took my pint and headed for the stairs.

My glass cracked.

In the corridor were photographs of past landlords and ladies. Unposed, they were the best sort of photographs, almost accidental in composition, catching the inconsequential moment that says more about a time gone by than any more formal, Sunday best, smile-at-the-camera professional portrait could hope to reveal. Those pictured were undoubtedly Characters, silently vying with each other for the biggest capital 'C'. Although I knew none of their stories, I felt that the building did, even if it wasn't telling. I was captivated by the pale features, animated within the undatable shadows - the same gas-lit shadows in which I now stood. The dark-waistcoated gentleman eyed me seriously across the years, the high-collared woman looked beyond the frame into a past I will never know.

My glass cracked. That's all.

The long room upstairs was ranked with stiff-backed chairs at functional tables. There was a piano in the corner, although it seemed inappropriate that it should sound. Downstairs, perhaps, could carry a beery 'Knees Up, Mother Brown', but this dressed itself as a room for more serious occasions. I could imagine workers gathered round to be 'improved' or just to grumble and plot in the grey-gold glow of the elaborate mantles. How many Woodbine dog-ends, I wondered, had been flung into the grate that guttered bravely at one end of the room, struggling to warm the shadows? And we had gathered for the last night of the Beverley Literature Festival, surely a worthy enough cause to break the silence. Open Mic night without the mic – five minutes and you're off, declaiming, stuttering, tragic, comic, rhyming or free. And, in between, time for new acquaintances and re-filling the glasses, joining the unending conversations that have animated these shadows since before I was born and will go on long after I've passed.

My glass cracked. That's all that happened.

Yes, it's as simple as that. In a lull in the conversation of the evening, of four centuries or more, my glass – not quite empty, on the table, untouched - cracked. With a clear crack like water scalding ice, a line drew across the side, three inches from the top. A second snap and the circle was complete. Silence and the shadows looked on. There are, no doubt, explanations, but I don't want to know them, because in that moment it wasn't just my glass, but time that cracked. The suspect lines between past and present, between myself and those in the photographs, that had looked so transparent and insubstantial since I first entered, finally gave way, leaving only the solidity of the building itself intact. Or so I like to think.

My glass cracked. That's all that happened. Glass cracked. ⁄⁄

Alan Gillott

Immortality

How confusing it must be
To be dead, yet still alive
Sustained in the fertile world
Of historical fiction
Hysterical works of literary imagination
Where eponymous heroes, lovers and villains
Real and imaginary
Influence or are influenced by
Famous men and women
In deeds they may or may not have done
Where in this Tinkerbelle reality
Minds we remember for their clarity
Caesar, da Vinci, Alexander,
Plato, Helen, Elizabeth, Ariadne,
Remember now similar words
Different people in different places
At the exact same time
Intimate friendships
Grotesque in their timing
At odds with honour yet not dishonourable
A puzzle that must befuddle
An added dimension to fame
Without the amnesia of dementia. ⁄⁄

Michael Hildred

The Water Meadow

In a quirk of radiant morning light
the little group is always there ahead;
indistinct, ethereal, glancing neither left
nor right. They are totally absorbed, lost
in conversation, slowly covering ground beside
the shallow gleaming stream; never looking back.

Then gentle shifts in ambience bring
startling revelation. The group comes into focus
and I'm staring at my son. So much taller
than the others, he's the centre of attention,
as they all veer round an obstacle of pink
festooning willowherb; never looking back.

I pause and so by chance do they, sorting
out the way ahead, taking in the view. It all
resembles Norfolk, with cottages of Norfolk pink
beneath a fenland sky. Yet I don't know how I got
here - and who are these people with my son,
as the stream goes rippling by; never looking back?

I'm closer now. The feeling grows that Patrick knows
I'm here. His companions start to move away,
obscured by drifts of willowherb; but he, stands clear.
Slowly, he turns around and looks at me, lighting
up his ready smile. It lingers, with a reassuring
wave, an outstretched hand suspended in the air.

That is the last time that I see him.
That is how I visualize him now;
always looking back at me across the water meadow;
and smiling. ⁄⁄

Val Horner

Nocturne

The curtains are drawn,
gauze rises and falls,
fingering grey light,
from a street, asleep

where dust lifts and stirs,
on scuffed passageways;
worn stones absorb,
the lingering heat. Seen

from the corner of an eye,
hovering shapes
ossify. Slowly rays
of a drifting moon, bleach

shadows from a wall,
shrinking hands pluck
the yellowing sheet,
gauze fingers, clutch and squeeze. ⫽

Andy Humphrey
Featherblack Redbeak

August 5th

Dear Helen,

Your husband's life ended at a place called Gauger's Leap. It is a small clifftop clearing on the remotest corner of a Scottish island which I do not intend to name. The place doesn't appear in any of the guidebooks. A hillwalker with the right Ordnance Survey map can find the place easily enough, but there is nothing on the map to mark it out as remarkable. On a clear day you can see as far as Ireland, hear the cries of choughs on the ledges below.

The islanders know it as a suicide spot. Jumping from Gauger's Leap has a grim finality to it. There's nothing below but a drop into empty space, and then black, skull-crushing rocks. Two or three poor bastards use it as their exit from life every year.

I still can't believe that Malcolm was one of them.

The coroner agreed that an accident was unlikely. There was enough evidence of what he'd been through in the last year, everything he'd lost. You would know that better than anyone. But suicide? Really? Not Malcolm.

The ferry will dock in a few minutes' time. I'll check into the hotel, have a whisky in the bar. I wonder if the place has changed at all?

Always,

Your loving brother

August 6th

Dear Helen,

I remember the first time Malcolm and I set foot on this island. That long, lazy summer after our first year, the summer before he met you. We hitch-hiked up from Oxford, brought a fold-away tent. He fell in love with the wildness of it. The unpredictable weather, the vastness of the sky.

We spent a week trying to ferret out where the choughs roosted. A local in one of the pubs tipped us off about Gauger's Leap.

The noise of them was astonishing. Their *chow, chow,* reverberating around the cliffs. The tumble and hurtle of their flight. I remember Malcolm standing on the clifftop with arms outstretched, his face turned up to the sky, exulting in their presence. I remember him telling me they were laughing at the clouds.

I can still remember the way he looked at you, the day the two of you met. You'd come to visit me for open day, an escape from the grind of study. You'd had some disaster with the hair dye a week before, and had this scarf wrapped tight around your head. I teased you, told you you looked like a hippie charlady. But Malcolm was smitten. You kissed that night, while I pretended not to look. You were seventeen, and you'd already sealed his fate.

I laughed when you told me you'd taken up ornithology. You were trying to impress him. But you never really needed to.

Please don't think he didn't love you. You were his world, you and Christopher. I can remember the light in his eyes when he knew that the two of you had another on the way, after all the years of trying, all the disappointments. And I've never seen him cry, the way he did when the doctors told him baby Eliza hadn't made it. It broke his heart, to lose her like that at the moment of her birth. And then – well, you know what happened then. How the melancholy took hold of him, drove him back out to these wild places we hadn't walked in years.

There's one more ritual left to perform. I'm ready, now.

Always,

Your loving brother.

August 7th

Dear Helen,

Colossal rainstorm today. The wind is throwing seagulls and crows about the sky like rags. Haven't dared venture out to Gauger's Leap. There'll be time for that tomorrow.

You know why they call it Gauger's Leap, of course.

Two hundred years ago there was an exciseman in these parts by the name of George Herrick. His job was to put an end to the illegal whisky trade that went on in the hills, fuelled by the peat beneath the moors. The stills were hidden in remote places, the whisky shipped to the mainland under cover of darkness.

George Herrick came to the island with the King's warrant, a team of Glasgow thugs at his back. One by one they tracked down the local stills and put them to the torch. They were none too discriminating about the bodies they left behind. George Herrick turned a blind eye to murder when he was about the King's business.

It was a late summer's night when he met his end. The free-traders would wait for a squally, stormy day before they sent their boats to the island. They came ashore under cover of darkness, landed at hidden coves where the stillmen and their accomplices would load them up with liquor. Only this night, Herrick got there first. He shot the drayman who was carting the whisky, found the signal fire on the landing-beach and put to death the men who were tending the fire. He quenched the signal fire and built his own on the cliff up at Gauger's Leap, a false signal to lure the boat onto the rocks.

There was a girl who saw what happened. A dark slip of a thing, daughter of one of the farming families. Her father and two of her brothers died at Herrick's hands that night. She found their bodies on the landing-beach, followed the trail up onto the cliffs.

The locals reckon one of the distillers had had a tip-off that Herrick was coming for them. The tale they tell on the island is that he'd tainted the barrels with foreshots from the still. In those days they didn't know about methanol, or toxic impurities, but they knew that the foreshots of a distillation were dangerous spirits, apt to turn a man to madness.

The Glasgow thugs had taken a cask from the drayman's cart. Up on the soaked and windswept cliff, they opened the barrel, drank from it while the free-traders' boat was wrecked on the rocks. The girl who watched them saw a fight break out, saw pistols being drawn, shots fired. Nowadays, we'd say they were hallucinating. When the girl told the tale, she said that the spirits of the men they'd murdered had come for them. Shapes out of the mist, swirling and snatching.

That was when George Herrick, faced with spectres at his back or black rocks beneath, launched himself over the edge.

The place had a bad reputation afterwards. Local folklore told how the ghosts of Herrick's victims would stalk the cliffs on foggy nights, reaching out for strangers just as they'd reached for Herrick and his men. The girl who saw Herrick leap onto the rocks came to a sad end. Maddened by grief for her family, she threw herself off the cliff not many months later. The story goes that her body snagged on a gorse bush halfway down the cliff, and her body dangled there for months. Eventually all that was left was a black shawl and the twist of red headscarf she'd worn over her hair. *Featherblack Redbeak*, the locals nicknamed her: the poor mad girl, plummeting from the cliffs like the choughs who roost there. Trying to fly away.

I don't suppose the ghosts lingered when the engineers came. There are radio transmitters along the cliff path now, mobile phone masts. But Gauger's Leap is unspoilt; a site of special scientific interest for the sake of the choughs.

They have a helicopter now. A man on a winch recovered Malcolm's body. No danger of him being caught like poor Featherblack Redbeak, denied the dignity of a proper funeral.

Always,

Your loving brother

August 8th

Dear Helen

The deed is done. Today I returned to Gauger's Leap to scatter Malcolm's ashes. To set him free on the wind, to fly like the choughs into a vertigo of sky. I opened that bottle of expensive malt we'd saved for Eliza's christening, sloshed it down my throat, and emptied the rest over the cliff edge. One final toast.

There was someone watching us from along the cliff. A dark shape with a splash of red at her head.

Maybe it was the whisky addling my brain, but there was something in her bearing told me that she didn't belong there. A flash of recollection, the story of Featherblack Redbeak fluttering in the wind. The ghosts of Gauger's Leap, come to welcome one more to their number.

"Wait!" I cried into empty air. The wind that had snatched away Malcolm turned my voice into a reedy, pathetic squeal. A moment later I was down the path towards her, reaching out and begging: *please don't go.* But there was no one there. Just an empty path, a chough taking flight with a clatter of wings.

The fogs that bedevil that end of the island are treacherous things. Often they're nothing more than clouds rising up off the surface of the sea. They can snatch and swirl around you with no warning, until suddenly you can hardly see the path in front of you, hardly know which way is safety and which way the edge of the cliff.

I got it wrong. My foot slipped, spun in space.

I snatched at a stubble of hawthorn on the edge of the cliff. Somehow I managed to arrest my fall. I was suspended, between sky and rock.

Hawthorn prickles burned into my hands. And just for an instant I found myself wondering what it would be like to let go. To be one with the air and the tumbling choughs. With Malcolm.

The hands that fastened on me were not strong, but they were insistent. With their help I was able to drag my way back to the path. My clothes were torn, my hands bleeding. My head pounded as if it would break open any minute. In wearied agony, I sank to my knees and let dizziness overtake me.

I just had time to make out the face that smiled at me through the mist. The girlish curl of a mouth, the flutter of raven hair beneath the scarlet headscarf. Then I knew.

You knew too, didn't you, Helen? Why he came here on that last journey.

He was looking for you.

Always,

Your loving brother

August 9th

Dear Helen,

It's such a cold, passionless word, don't you think? *Preeclampsia*. It happens to pregnant women all the time. It shouldn't be fatal. Not in this day and age.

It's no comfort to know you were just the one in a hundred thousand. It was certainly no comfort to Malcolm. His eyes still wet with the loss of Eliza, and then to hear that you'd left him too...

Part of me couldn't help thinking it wasn't quite right, carrying Malcolm's ashes all that way, without carrying you too. But he'd been very clear about that. There needed to be a place where Chris could come and remember his mother. A gravestone, a rose bush, a tree, it didn't really matter. What mattered was that he could touch it, be connected to your life somehow by the sense of what you'd left behind.

Malcolm, though – Malcolm was pure air.

He really was looking for you, that final journey. Knew that he'd find you on the clifftop, flying with the choughs. Waiting. All he wanted was to be with you again.

And me? Well, I'm peaceful now. I've recaptured the light in your eyes, the curl of the smile of the little-girl Helen, the sister I danced with and teased, whose hair I used to pull. That's enough for me now.

I could have let go, yesterday on the cliff. But you wouldn't let me.

There's Christopher to think of now. He'll be starting secondary school next month. I bet you never thought he'd grow up so fast.

I'll bring him here, one day not too far off. We'll fling our arms open and laugh at the clouds.

Always,

Your loving brother ⫽

Martin Huxter

The Shadow on the Stairs

Some just brought ideas, vague notions,
others held finished poems neatly typed.

Some read private thoughts with a trembling voice,
or bellowed stanzas blasphemous and long.

One young man had reams of verse held back for weeks,
then gradually aired each one and sprouted wings.

The confident argued, defended their stance,
while others caved-in to the slightest doubt.

A handful knew she valued poets above all,
and thought her at least the equal of her man.

Each one brought with them their hopes and dreams,
though none, I think, would have them realized.

A few, whose verse disappointed week in week out,
would have made better priests than poets.

And it's possible depending on which definitions you use,
that some gained entry who were not, and never would be, bards.

I think just one saw the shadow on the stairs,
and, though it was not malign, felt the slightest chill.

Some brought gifts: old books or wine,
others came burdened only by their woes.

Most just picked at the offered buffet;
one man devoured with relish like an ogre's friend.

Those with good breeding read the wine label first;
most quaffed steadily without enquiry.

The to-ings and fro-ings were noted by neighbours,
though hints of subversion were mostly ruled out.

On the way there some saw the sky filled with birds
and knew it must have been the same back then.

Some saw crows and thought of ravens;
a few thought beggars resembled pigeons.

At the door they looked up at all the feathers
and searched the gutter for filigree bones.

Only one, I think, saw the shadow on the stairs
and felt a slight chill, though it was most benign.

Some had a haunted or hunted look
and all were somewhat sad of eye.

None had troubadour tights or sauntered like minstrels;
there were the unshaven, the dapper and the down at heel.

One or two had jackets of the finest suede,
others wore soiled trench coats, all threads and patches.

There were the earnest and the lazy;
those who scurried and those who crept.

Some came with a spring, an optimistic stride
and left muttering and reeling like a pisshead tramp.

Only one, I think, saw the shadow swelling,
as if enriched and gaining strength.

The nervous fumbled frantically for the passage light,
others strode boldly through darkness to the street.

Several encouraged friends to join,
a few left vowing never to come again.

One or two hurried along the canal before the U-bahn closed,
or took a winding route, dropping into desperate bars.

Some noticed girls in dimly lit doorways
and, though feeling pity, moved briskly on.

Only one, I think, followed the shadow upstairs
and heard it mouth softly, "Yellow Street." ⚏

Martin Huxter

Old Miss Bartram

Miss Bartram gave her name to a squid
O bartrami and came back from the dead
a skeleton walking walking dead
old skeleton in a russet dress
shaking rattling ramshackle bones
I saw Miss Bartram come back from the dead
kindly toy calf head rubbed three days dead
tent-pole dislocate dinosaur hump
her bones came clattering down the street
russet day-coat, apron, dress.

Miss Bartram gave her name to a squid
a huge tall woman though somewhat bent
knit bullet-proof cosies for church bazaars
rhubarb raspberry lemon curd
dove dived when she wasn't doing this
for still undiscovered deep-sea squid
Victoria Sandwich trembling hands
Miss Bartram came knocking back from the dead
ramshackle rattling rubbed-off skull head
russet day-coat, apron, dress. //

*A child's account of seeing an old lady out walking three days after she died.

41

Helen Burke

Our Viking Lodger

Eastenders is his thing.
Our Viking lodger.
He fancies Stacey - dreams of being Bradley.
Max and Tania - real good Vikings he says.
They try to kill each other.
Several times in the one episode.
Fantastic.
The children all drink and smoke.
Excellent, - he beams.
He twinkles with delight as people
are bumped off around the square.
He wants to marry Peggy Mitchell.
A fine woman - he croons.
So small - and yet, so vicious.
Her sons are honorary Vikings, he says.
Grant - the Great Absent One - and
Phil - the Alky Unready.
Dot Cotton is a Viking Soothsayer. She breathes so much fire -
he is in awe.
Shirley and Heather are Valkyries. Their souls tormented
and warrior like.
The laundrette is a secret portal into Valhalla.
Little Billy Mitchell - even he is blessed with the Holy Rune.
Ian Beal is Loki - when he cries - he throws lager cans at the
screen.
Why does Jane stay ?? he screams.   Why ??
By the time he watches the Omnibus on Sunday - he is calmer.
We see his helmet horns twitching with joy as
Ronni stares into the space above Jack's head and Roxy
forgets her lines again, and chews yet another piece of gum.
His dreams are full of Janine - serving him blueberry mead.
His nightmares are full of Pat Butcher - doing the same. ⁄⁄

Second Seat at Seagulls

"It's down by the river. Seagulls. I can't believe that you have never seen it."

Hazel shook her head. "No. No, I'm sorry. You say that it is opposite the cinema?"

Billy moved, to sit next to her, and pointed to the door, then indicating left. "Well, sort of. I guess that if you don't know it, then it's more difficult than I'm making it sound." Billy felt it impossible to smile as he felt Hazel's hand just touch his, brushing it. This first date might well go well, he was beginning to realise.

"If you come out of the cinema, you only need to go across the road, then through the little alleyway, and Seagulls is down there. I will meet you in the second seat, as you walk in. You wouldn't see Seagulls from the cinema, I guess, but you can certainly see it when you get in to the alleyway – it's about ten yards, and then on the left."

Hazel smiled. "I'm sure I can find it. It sounds very simple to find."

Billy nodded. "It is. I will see you there tonight, at about six?" Hazel nodded, in agreement.

"Yes. Yes, definitely. About six."

"Great. Right, I had better head back to work. Any problems, just give me a call on the mobile, and I'll see you a little later."

Hazel smiled as Billy stood, heading to the door, and waving as he left. Billy realized that he was going to be a fraction late for work, but that it might all be worthwhile.

Billy sat in the second seat in Seagulls. He was a little early, and very nervous. He was struggling to believe that Hazel had agreed to meet him – that she had agreed, essentially, to go *on a date* with him. Maybe she thought it

43

was – no. Do not think like that, he told himself. Hazel *had* agreed to go on a date with him. She was beautiful, intelligent, and she clearly liked him.

Just get on with it, he thought. Enjoy the night. Just enjoy it. There may not be another night like this. Enjoy.

He leaned back on the second seat, and waited.

Hazel stood outside the cinema, a little early and very nervous. She could not believe that she was going out with Billy. She had liked him for ages, but never thought. No, she told herself. Enjoy the night.

There were two alleyways opposite the cinema. Billy had not mentioned that. She wanted to head down the correct alleyway. Why was there another alleyway? Why was she worried about the alleyways?

She smiled. She was not worried about the alleyways – she was worried about the date. Was it a date? Yes. Yes, it was a date. She looked over the road. The bigger, brighter alleyway looked much more like the one she was supposed to be heading for. The other one just seemed to be the backs of houses, but it was difficult to say.

The bigger alleyway was on the right. That would have to be the one to go for. That would be ok, she would just head in that direction, over the road, and everything...

oh, no.

Seagulls was quiet, again. She had not seen or heard 'William' in the past few weeks, but that was not going to bring people back – at least, not straight away. She had not been 'aware' of him for quite some time, but she knew he had not left permanently. There was something about. Well.

He'd been quieter, though, not that that was bringing people back in. He'd moved glasses just a little recently, and the presence was still forbidding in the area of the second seat at Seagulls. He had not been nasty in the way that he had when she had first taken over Seagulls. She wondered why the pub had been so cheap, and it had only taken her a

44

week to find out. He had moved glasses, tables – he had even thrown a chair at one point, the one next to the second seat in.

Roz wondered how much of the story she had found out about William was true. William had been waiting for someone, a regular had told her. She had not seen that regular for a little while now, but she had not seen anybody for a little while.

William was waiting for his love, on the second seat in, apparently. The girl had never arrived – she had been killed before she got there. When he had discovered this, William had thrown himself off the cliff so close to here, down the next alleyway. Now he was waiting, and it looked as if he would be waiting forever.

Roz sat down on the first chair and looked around at her deserted pub, sighing.

"It's just you and me now, William," she said. "Everyone else has gone, and you know that she is never going to get here. She's gone, and it's nobody's fault. It's time that you headed home too, I think. I'm sorry. Nobody is coming for me, either – nobody comes in to Seagulls at all any more, you can see that. Is that what you wanted? Nobody is going to come here if you don't go. It's closing time, Billy, for both of us."

Roz wondered if William was listening, and was surprised at her strength to talk to him now.

"Please, Billy, head home. Nobody is going to meet anybody if you stay. I'm not, and your date is not going to be here. It's not her fault, it's nobody's fault. It's closing time, for both of us."

Roz stood, and walked to switch the lights off. She had a strange sense that she was being listened to, so she had to finish this, and finish it now.

"I'm going home to bed now. If you go, people can meet up again in Seagulls. If you stay, nobody will meet up. There will be no more chances. Tonight, it is time to go. When I come back tomorrow, I'll be looking after this place without you. You've got to let me do that. Is that ok?"

45

Roz paused, knowing that nothing would –

'*yes.*'

No. No. She had not heard that –

She *had* heard that. She smiled, and nodded.

"Thank you, Billy. Thank you. Goodnight. Sleep well."

Roz turned out the lights and headed home, realizing that tomorrow morning, Seagulls was going to become a good place to meet again. ⁄⁄

Robin Lewis
York, New York

I took one picture of my friend when we went to New York.
    She is on a boat and we are heading over to Liberty
Island, and

it is a sunny day and

in the background you can see
    two towers standing tall and

she is smiling. ⁄⁄

Steve Nash

Hutch

As I made my lonely way home from school,
in short grey trousers, unhappy,
uncool,
my mind fell away to a wishing zone
where I longed for a friend or a pet
of my own.

As I loped through the door I knew something had changed,
my tired parents were grinning, in itself this
was strange.
"There's a surprise for you out the back, nothing much."
I ventured outside and found
the hutch.

My eyes double-taked, my heart skipped a beat;
a rabbit of my own, to talk to,
to keep.
In the shadow of the shed the hutch was pitch black
through the dizzying blackness two amber eyes
stared back.

"Will you be my friend Mr Rabbit?" I asked.
"Possibly," came a snarl. "First complete me
a task.
I'm ever so hungry, I haven't eaten for days.
Why not rustle up some food boy, then bring it
my way?"

With a song in my heart I bounced into the pantry.
"Thanks Mum and Dad, is there food for my
bunny?"
My arms overflowing with veg without end
I ran back past the shed to feed my
new friend.

The amber eyes flashed - my pet was displeased.
"What the hell is this boy? Don't believe all
you read!
Us rabbits don't enjoy carrots, lettuce and cress,

what really excites us is the sweet taste
of flesh."

"Hmm," I pondered, "I'll see if my folks have some meat.
But honest, I promise this is what they said
you'd eat."
The amber eyes brightened, "Parents you say?
Why not do me a task boy and bring them
my way?"

Without a moment's pause I rushed back to the house.
"My bunny wants to see you guys, quickly,
right now!"
With puzzled expressions in their weary, old eyes
my folks slowly dragged their hefty backsides
outside.

"Why have you moved him over there by the shed?
Did you open the hutch door? Why's the grass
all red?"
Dad's questions were silenced by a shriek from my mother
who'd noticed my bunny as it emerged from its
cover.

"You don't look like a rabbit, not from the pictures I've seen."
"I told you boy," it answered. "Don't believe all
you read."
It stalked steadily towards us on its great four paws.
It bared its huge teeth and glittering
claws.

In just a couple of moments my parents were gone.
He'd devoured them whole except the hair from
my Mum.
As he flossed his red teeth with her, once flaxen, strands
he peered down at me, smiled and then took
my hand.

"Tell me my boy is anyone else there indoors?"
"Only my sister," I sighed, "I hate her,
she's four."
Through his bristling, black fur my bunny smiled wide.
"Call me Flopsy," he said. "Now lets go
inside." ⁄⁄

49

Dick Ockelton
Low Spirits

Here we go again, the usual tedium.
"Why are you restless, Spirit?" asks the medium.
Why <u>does</u> she keep asking? She already knows.
I've told her before. It's the state of my clothes.

In the land of the living, as a fashion designer,
My dress was impeccable. Nobody finer.
So think how it felt. I could not have been sadder,
Than meeting my end when I fell off a ladder,
In paint-spattered clothes and my knees through my jeans,
And old Nike trainers I've had since my teens.

I can't meet my Maker in togs such as these.
What should I be wearing? Oh, Armani please!
But no, in my scruff, I just waft around here,
With a headless princess and the odd Cavalier.
Just look at their finery. Puts me to shame.
OK, they've no heads, but they're smart just the same.

And if that's not enough, just to add to it all,
The paint stains are Homebase, not Farrow and Ball.
Is it too much to ask, for crying out loud?
The ones who die naked at least get a shroud,
With long flappy sleeves and the eyeholes cut out,
So they can go haunting and howling about.

If I was a Buddhist, I'd not feel so low.
At least as a Buddhist I'd get one more go.
I'd wear my best suit and just die at a wedding.
But Buddhist I'm not, and the chance of me shedding
My nemesis garb is not within reach,
So I'll weep and I'll wail and continue to screech.

Maybe going to Hell's a solution of sorts.
At least it's so hot, I could just wear my shorts.
(Calvin Klein of course). ∥

Gabrielle de Yorvick

Fog

Dark, dank, early morning. The bus depot is silent and deserted. Thick fog shrouds the buildings and blurs the dividing line between road and pavement. It lurks in the doorways, in the bushes, round the single lamp post and makes shadow monsters in the corners. A lone Routemaster, 36B, stands waiting, like a forgotten toy, its fog misted windows glinting eerily in the half light.

Muffled footsteps. Sean walks slowly toward the bus-park, his head throbbing with the memory of last night's argument. He glances around, the place is empty. Typical: the one day on which he wants to be anywhere but here, has to be the one day when everything is transfixed by the damn fog. A two mile walk is not normally how he would start his day, but he could not have stayed there, not even for half an hour more. He had to get away. His suitcase drips fog onto his shoes as his feet begin to ache in sympathy with his head. He looks toward the buildings, hoping for a seat somewhere, but all he sees are black rubbish sacks, torn and spewing their contents onto the path. Best not to dwell on what unseen teeth may have made the tears.

Sean turns, looks at the bus, and decides. Hurrying now, he throws his suitcase into the luggage hatch and makes his way to the driver's door. It is unlocked. Climbing in he checks for keys - under the mat? On the dashboard? A gleam of silver in the gear-shift well - Yes!

The engine starts, but the gears shift unbidden, the wheels roll forward. Sean panics; where is he going? Where can he go?

Slowly the bus moves out of the park, Sean tries to control it, tries to turn right - but unseen powers are controlling the steering. The bus turns left into the main street and gains momentum. He can see nothing through the windscreen, the fog is too dense. The lights don't work. The pedals don't work... Nothing responds to his touch. The bus is gathering speed and out of control... and then it is gone!

He is standing again in the bus park, suitcase in hand, dripping fog onto his shoes. Frightened, he tries to run but cannot move. A police siren stirs the fog, a blue flashing light distorts his vision.

"Sean Casey, I am arresting you for the murder of your wife, Yvonne Casey. You do not have to say anything, but anything you do say may be taken down and used in evidence."

They take his suitcase and open it. Her face smiles up at him from its bloodied depths. He had had to keep that smile - the rest didn't matter. A bus trundles by through the fog: 36B. ⁄⁄

Adrienne Odasso

Namesakes

1. Josephine

She died in your arms. Twenty-nine years gone,
and still the sting's as fresh as morning fog
on the rhubarb patch Great-Uncle Dave kept
in one corner of the wash-house garden.
Why you're telling me now, I can't fathom,
although part of me can guess: you grow frail
with the waning of the seasons, reasons
growing thick as those wild grapes on the vine
not far from where she fell. As you bore her,
Grandma, did you dream that eyes like ours
would ever light on yours again? Did the night-
turned-dawning when I entered this world
mark her passing, or did she, stubborn, remain?

2. Darla

I was six months old in your arms, you said,
when we found her. No answer at the door.
Circling the house for an hour, peering
in through drapes and blinds all veiling the bed.
You called her son, asked if he'd heard
from her lately. Even *one* ring? No, none.
Then came the rain, the ambulances' wail
pricks upon my skin, twirl of your fine hair
through tiny fingers. They said she'd been gone
at least two days, had kissed the pills
and lain her down to sleep. I don't wonder
which traces of grief were tears, which the storm.
My purpose here has been to watch you mourn. //

PJ Quinn

The Devil's Hand

"Surely, Reverend, *you* don't believe in ghosts?"

Malcolm's laughter gave way to silence. The Local History Group looked at the Vicar in surprise.

At first the clergyman didn't reply. He walked to the window and looked towards the spire of his church, nestling between two huge oak trees.

Finally, the Vicar turned to the group. "I should warn you off this line of research," he started, "but to do so would give way to superstition and rumour. Just keep an open mind and be very careful. You could open a box of secrets that should remain shut."

David opened his mouth to interject, but the Vicar continued. "Your starting point might as well be the grave. If you follow me I'll show you where it is. It's still light enough."

Puzzled, the group followed the Vicar, hurrying behind him like parishioners late for mass. They entered the graveyard, turning right into the furthest corner. The graves here were the oldest. Stone lions keep silent guard. Frozen cherubim stared towards wilted roses. Someone had tied a red ribbon round an old white cross.

Passing a large angel on a marble plinth, the Vicar turned towards the wall. There, almost hidden, the group found a small grave, mottled grey and green.

"If you don't mind, I'll leave you here," the Vicar turned away. "I suggest you don't stay too long. It will be dark soon."

"And I'd advise you not to touch the grave," he added. "Strange things happen to those who do." A couple of the group shuddered as they watched him go.

"That's odd, don't you think?" It was David who spoke first. "This grave looks ancient, but the date seems to be 1919."

"Perhaps it's 1819?" Rebecca said.

"No, the dates are definitely 1895 to 1919," Gerry replied. "He wasn't very old when he died."

"What was he called?" Sally pushed forwards for a closer look.

"Presumably," Rita pointed out, "he was called Villiers. After all, Villiers Park was named after him."

"It's not what the grave says," Malcolm swallowed slightly. "I'd swear it says 'Sir Joseph Devil'!"

He bent down for a better look. Forgetting the Vicar's warning, Malcolm ran his fingers over the withered stone. He was surprised at how warm and enticing it felt. Suddenly he jumped as he felt a heavy hand on his right shoulder. He glanced over but there was no one there. Shrugging, Malcolm looked back at the grave.

"It seems to have been changed at some point," he said. "It looks like someone's added the letters 'D' and 'e' at the beginning and tried to scrub off the 'liers' at the end. Now why on earth would someone do that?" Malcolm raised his head to look at the others.

"Maybe," Rebecca replied quietly, "someone was trying to make a point?"

"That's it, just take it slowly," Kathy held her father's arm gently. She paused to let him catch his breath.

She'd been taking him for his walk for nearly a year now, ever since his stroke: since he'd no longer been able to walk alone or, for that matter, to choose where to go each afternoon. Villiers Park, opposite the nursing home, was perfect: easy to get to, with plenty of benches for her father to rest on.

They took their usual route, past the tennis courts to the ornamental pond. Then they stopped, as they did every day, to look at the small golden fish. In spring they'd seen tadpoles and later watched the tiny frogs hopping away.

Kathy turned but was surprised when her father didn't move. He was still staring at the pond. She followed his gaze, straining her eyes to see if he'd spotted one of the little newts that skulked along the bottom. The still water reflected the sky above, the clouds skidding across the surface. Then Kathy saw the water-sky darken, the clouds growing in size, an ominous green-black. Another face suddenly appeared, mirrored right next to hers: an oval face, pale and female. The woman was crying.

Kathy was puzzled. She hadn't heard the woman approach, or her sobbing.

Looking up, Kathy found herself staring into thin air. Perplexed, she turned back to her father, but he was still staring at the pond. Glancing back at the water, she saw again the reflection of the sad, weeping lady; except the only person near was her father.

Kathy was silent as she took her father home.

It was a whim that brought her out again to the park. She knew where her feet were taking her before she even got to the pond. Kathy leant against the railings, scrutinising the water carefully. She knew her mind must have been playing tricks. She could hardly ask her father what he'd seen. Even if he hadn't lost the power of speech, he would have probably made no sense. He'd had early-stage dementia even before the stroke.

Kathy had no problem believing in the supernatural. She'd listened to friends' stories of ghostly sightings with regret. She'd hoped one day she might see for herself whether spirits did exist. It made her feel better to think that her father's soul might still be intact, within the barely functioning physical host.

She had been daydreaming for some time, staring intently at the pond. She hadn't even noticed the face appear next to hers.

Kathy came to with a start. There was absolutely no doubt that she was looking at another woman's mirror-face, right next to hers. The woman had stopped sobbing but tears still streaked her cheeks. Kathy didn't need to turn her head to know that she was alone at the pond. She tried to remain calm. On an impulse, she spoke to the reflection. It seemed the right thing to do. Of course, she realised that anyone seeing her would have thought her mad: staring at the water, talking to herself. She also realised she had absolutely no idea what to say to a ghost.

She finally decided on a simple "Hello". The pale reflection turned its head to acknowledge her.

Astonished, Kathy tried again. "Is there anything I can do to help?" This time the head shook.

Again Kathy ran out of things to say. Finally she asked "are you going to be alright if I leave you?"

The reflection paused. There was a slight shrug of the shoulders. Kathy realised she could now see more of the woman. She was dressed in white muslin, like an old-fashioned summer dress; the type Kathy's grandmother would have worn as a girl. The woman was young and beautiful. She wore her blond hair up away from her face, flattering her delicate cheekbones. Kathy was suddenly struck by their likeness. She could have been looking at her much younger, prettier sister. It was no wonder her father had been so confused.

As Kathy stared at the reflection, a hand appeared at its neck: a male hand, gloved and large. The hand disappeared but Kathy understood. The lady had been strangled.

"Oh my God!" Kathy couldn't help it; the words tumbled out. "Did they catch who did this to you?"

The woman shook her head. "But do you know who he was?" Kathy was insistent. The woman nodded, starting to cry again.

"There must be something I can do to help. I can try to make sure he's punished," Kathy exclaimed.

"Don't worry," a male voice said behind her. "He'll probably be punished for eternity."

Wheeling round, Kathy came face to face with the Vicar. "I see you've met Ellen," he added.

"So what makes you so sure?" David asked as they walked through the park. It had been raining heavily; the ground was soft beneath their feet. A flock of seagulls was trying to out-screech the crows.

"Sir Joseph Villiers was injured in the Great War," Malcolm replied. "When he got back his fiancée, Ellen Longbottom, disappeared. I think Joseph killed her and then committed suicide. Either that or he was lynched by the local mob for her murder. He was so hot-tempered, he was known locally as 'The Devil' even before the War."

"He was probably suffering shell shock," David said. "But she may just have left him. You can't be certain he killed her."

They were walking down a tree-lined path, towards old Villiers Hall. Despite being turned into tiny flats, the building was still beautiful. Malcolm stopped in the shade of two ancient chestnut trees, their gnarled bark covered in green lichen.

"This is the oldest part of the park," Malcolm dropped his voice. He wasn't sure why he was whispering.

He found himself walking towards another tree, so large its trunk had split in two. Both sides twisted upwards, supported by wooden stakes. He saw with surprise that absolutely nothing was growing beneath: the ground was a barren brown. One of the wooden supports had pulled out of the ground. The soft earth seemed to have lost its hold. Stepping forward, Malcolm glanced down. He immediately wished he hadn't. A flash of white caught his eye. He was looking at a skull.

"How the hell did you know she was buried here?" David whistled quietly in astonishment.

Malcolm flushed slightly. He couldn't explain what had happened last night. How he'd not just visualised strangling the young lady, how he actually felt himself doing it. How he'd watched from above as he buried her body under a tree. Or how he'd woken in a sweat just as the noose was tightening around his neck. "I had a dream," was all he said.

Kathy stood in the graveyard, looking at the tombstone she'd just paid for. It simply stated *"RIP, found at last."* She had wanted to add Ellen's name, but the Vicar pointed out they couldn't be sure the skeleton was hers.

He had queried Kathy's other request too; that Ellen's ashes be placed near the body of her former fiancé. It was a strange choice, the Vicar felt, but finally he'd agreed. He wasn't sure Kathy was right, though, that putting them together would lay their ghosts to rest.

"I wonder if you can forgive a man, in death, who took your life?" Kathy mused out loud.

"Let's hope so," the Vicar replied. "I think they both deserve to lie in peace."

Kathy smiled, putting a hand out to touch the new gravestone. She was surprised how warm it felt yet a shiver went down her spine. Suddenly she felt dizzy and lightheaded. As she held on to the grave tightly for support, she felt a small, dainty hand on her shoulder.

"Are you alright, Kathy?" the Vicar sounded concerned.

She turned to look at him in surprise. "Why do you call me Kathy?" she asked. "My name's Ellen." ⁄⁄

Helen Sant
Ghosts

They hang on still waters
then disappear among the lake lillies;
folding under shadows of moonless sky
and clinging to the daydreams of tomorrow's rumours.
Are they promises of eternal life
beyond the mason's stone
and scattered ash?
Or are they unbottled stories
longing for release
waiting to be told
late into the night
in the attic of never? ⁄⁄

Adrian Spendlow

Invisible Child

A child of the village that no one would know
Grey as the ashes, he scarcely could grow
Old are his clothes and ill fitting indeed
Is said that his skin is impossible to bleed
'Bad blood tis what did it,' say some thereabout
Some, that it all long before tumbled out
But the boy, if he boy be, for timeless an age
Has hollowly wandered, his own self as a cage
Grey as the death that he lives in alone
No one befriends, not the fool or the crone
Hardly is he noticed this invisible child
Not one with the living, askance of the wild
He does have abode, it is said, down the lane
But no one there heeds him or calls him a name
Rumour there was of a visitor inquisitive
Hapless traveller enquirer who watched where did live
"Nobody, no one, not here," came reply
Cold was the door opener and dead was the eye
Denying all knowledge of any such soul
Like all residents had done since Satan was old
'Was said that this visitor did ramble, was spent
A shadow himself, of all joy did repent
So never now notice the shadow child eye
Or you too invisible quickly will fly
Nor even look fleetingly at his back as he goes
For heart-brokenly lonely in your mind will impose
For ever then hapless, ill-fitting, unknown
Walks the boy of this village – unnoticed – alone ⫽

*From Essence of Ghost *available through www.adrianspendlow.co.uk

Paul Sutherland

Ma-ai
For L.M

In a past landscape
at a table, wishful, three guests
sat podding peas.

Each guest had someone
sitting close who was soundless
without shape or scent:

once foreseen futures
unfulfilled, negative space
no one could traverse

absent destinies
within reach of a hug
between place-settings. ⫽

Andrew Turnbull
Daily Routine

All our lives have a pattern of some sort,
All our days have a start and a stop,
Locations and situations and age,
Might modify our self replication.
Passions and pains, may burn some memories deep,
And other days we go through the motions.
Save for the door that sometimes stubs your toe,
Or the occasional unfamiliar,
Perfume you thought you just caught in the hall,
Or pipe tobacco by the garden shed,
On a wet autumn Sunday afternoon.

And Darren does not take too much notice,
These unremarkable things he lets go by,
Because rational Darren deals in facts.
A man on the bus in a demob suit?
It's a big city with all kinds of folk.
A brown dress lady kicking leaves in spring?
Live and let live, it's not against the law.
Of course! Darren sees them regularly.
He has a routine, they share his City,
And if there is one thing of which he is sure,
We underestimate coincidence.

The paranormal is just the normal,
Ascribing spirits in to your day,
Is mostly harmless delusional fun,
'A ghost is an emotional echo'?
What? Like a man on a bus in a suit
Who grieved to death in 1953?
Or the mother that kicked dry autumn leaves
With joy in her heart for her dear children.
Emotional memories burnt deep.

No, Darren won't have that, or spirits
Moving or perfuming things as messages
If he stubs his toe or smells tobacco
There'll be a rational explanation.

So Darren's career goes through its routines
And he denies all attempts at contact,
Ignoring the ghosts he sees every day,
Because being so haunted is not good for
A paranormal investigator. ⫻

Tanya Nightingale

Mappa Mundi
(after Philip Gross)

In the land where no-one lies
fiction is the first to go:
novels are bought under the counter
then radios, recorded speech.
Children learn permitted phrases:
It's perfect - yes thank you - that suits you - ask father –
and talk in their sleep.

In the land of constant light
young people go skiing at midnight
and lovers dance in the parks.
Old women walk under parasols,
bathe their eyes before bed
and dream of the scent of jasmine.

In the land of shifting ground
the cartographers are always busy.
People walk the streets in pairs
and conga-ing is common.
Even the stars are shiftless
and men's blood finds its echo in the seas.

In the land where no-one dies
citizens may possess only what they can carry.
Time too is rationed and pets forbidden.
Crowded around hearths,
women long for children
and men see new faces in the flames. //

Adrienne Odasso
Lost and Found

1. Bird Skull

Precious chick, I found you
when I walked waist-high
to morning-glory vines
and couldn't keep my eyes
above ground. There you lie,
fresh as dawn, cast in dew,
less than thought. Drops pooled
where breath once flooded
your beak. I bent and took you
in cupped hands, reverent,
sensing your soft, small spirit
as oh-so-startled it fled.

2. White Shell

So far inland, land-locked, past
the rough touch of forgiving sand
you sat in that self-same high grass,

not far from the hallowed place
of my poor hatchling's open grave.
You had a brother, dark, conical,

nothing to your clean, haunting curves.
I took you both home, pretended
that the ghosts of hermit crabs

lived in you. Filled you. Loved. ⁄⁄

Malin Bergström

The Metamorphosis

She whispers the key words to
the locked cat ears
accusing, hexing the shallow cackle
that bounces off the September moon.
And perhaps within that curly haired head of hers
all the songs finally begin to make
sense.

Heels that mark the floor varnish
with Braille words that come
from her colourful march.
Rashes the insides of her thighs
when the shattered night closes in
vegetating her to the floorboards
she slowly recalls
how to breathe.

The woman is not:
Complete Damaged Form
reshaped and mutilated.
She can play any role but is
inclined to escape
her plan to self-destruct or destroy,
or simply staying on the floor.
Attempting to voice without sound.
Attempting to purr. ⚅

Amina Alyal

Animal Supernatural

'Mythology is a disease of language...' Friedrich Max Müller.

Cold, he said.

It's the g'raffe, she said.

There's a g'raffe, coming in at the door.
Shall I close the door?

Poor giraffe, shut out, invisibly
pacing marble floors. Perhaps
one day it would show itself.

Perhaps, with luck, the goat would not.
I heard them whispering
they'd seen the goat.
No one wants to see that goat
just one smokey head floating,
because goats of that kind
have no body, I heard them say,
just misty, with no body.

Thoughts slide like wolves
dropping out of grey wool
blankets. Schiller and Freud
wink, and open the doors.
Words dance animal-masked in the carnival.

No one would say the mistletoe
should not be there on the oak.

Cut it, but hang it up: and watch the dancers

kiss new faces as the masks pass round. //

Pauline Kirk
Cavern

Before the hills grew smooth, I existed. For a million years
of your time - measureless in mine - water trickled
downwards. As it passed, it carved my caverns. Then, one
waking, the rock beneath me moved and my ways grew
deep.

I became a place of silences and sanctuary. In me, summer
and winter merged to an even coolness. My waters were
fresh. The great gash of my entrance gave shelter.

Bats found me first. In clouds as black as my walls, they
flew between me and the forests. Creeping things appeared
too, blind worms in my mud. Ferns began to grow in my
entrance, and along the gaps where light filtered from
above. Soon the big cats discovered me. For centuries I
watched their young at play. Then came the bears,
lumbering into my passageways, as deep as they dared.

Finally, creatures on two legs appeared. They climbed up
from the valley and cowered in my entrance, wrapped in
borrowed skins. My shelter pleased them. When their
predators had gone they stayed, lighting fires that kept us
both warm. Sometimes they would put their hands in the
yellow mud and press their palms against my walls; to leave
their mark they told me, and to honour my spirit. I needed
no such flattery. Beyond feeling, I watched as their young
strayed into my chasms. I would hear them calling, and
wonder why they could not fly like the bats.

Later, other two-legged creatures came. These people knew
colours and lines, and how to make dull rock glow. Wanting
to please me, they decorated my sides. Their magic brought
the animals I had sheltered onto my walls: tigers and bears,
horses, even birds. One young female could draw reindeer as
if they pranced before her. The other painters would stop to
watch, or bring her gifts of water and coloured clay. She
would draw strange creatures too, from the world outside I
had never seen: animals with slender necks or huge shaggy

bodies. As each one came alive, her companions would dance towards it, spears raised as if to kill, but she would not join them. For her, the pleasure was in the drawing itself.

I cannot remember when the painters left. A storm raged above me, and water gushed down through my rocks. Though the flood drained away, it left pools along my paths. A new stream flowed through me, sometimes a trickle, sometimes a raging torrent. For years my caves were silent again, but for the steady drip drip of water.

Outside, the light came and went. I dozed and woke, and dozed again. Each waking, the forests on the valley sides were thinner, the cries of bird and creature fainter. The hills grew bare, home only to woolly creatures that bleated. They sheltered under my canopy but gave nothing in return.

By then the two-legged painters lived with these animals. They liked to sit just inside me, eating the food they had brought. I began to understand their babble. They called themselves 'men' and 'women' and spoke as if they ruled the valley. Yet they were afraid of me. Some did enter, but they wished only to mate. Few explored my chambers. They were lucky to return. Parties of men with loud voices have come here several times, searching for some foolish youth lost within me. My silences should have warned them.

Again the light came and went over the valley. There were new sounds, distant thumps as of rock falling into sand, or a puffing that travelled up and down. With them came many new visitors. They peered into my opening and shouted to the echo, as irritating as a plague of insects.

Last wakening, different men came, stronger and quieter, showing no fear. They carried lights on their heads and knew how to crawl or wade through my tunnels. As they explored, they gave names to each of my features, as if they were the first to discover me. I listened to their conceit, and could not determine whether they came to hide or breed.

Suddenly, two of these people stumbled into my innermost cavern. They crouched in silence, looking upwards. One shone a light around my walls. He saw the paintings above him. "Tom!" he shouted.

"Oh, my God!"

Their voices echoed. For the first time since the painters left, I heard myself revered.

Finally they turned to leave. "We must tell Tony!" Tom said.

"No!" the other shouted back. "He'll have the Press in before you know it. Let's keep this to ourselves."

"Don't be stupid! This place will make us!"

Then they were gone.

Later - it seemed just a little while - the men returned. They brought another man and an older woman, weaker specimens, who needed help through my narrow ways. It took them a long time to struggle into my cavern. Standing beside the stream, they flashed their lights above them, backwards and forwards. Crying out in amazement they marvelled at so much darkness, so many deer and horses rushing through it. When they spoke, it was with joy.

"Let's get a closer look!" Tom said.

They had carried bundles through my waters, and they opened the wrappings. Inside were rods that they attached to the rocks. The man they called Dan seemed to be their leader. When he was satisfied, they fixed lights back onto their heads and began to climb. Painfully, slowly, as if weighed down by their clothing, they edged upwards. I did not understand why they found it so difficult. The people who painted the shapes they sought were not afraid of my darkness, nor of the height.

Finally they hauled themselves over the last rocks, and stood where the reindeer woman had stood. At first they seemed dumb or sleeping. When at last they woke, each spoke in a hushed voice.

"Incredible!" the woman whispered. She shone her light onto the rock. A sabre-toothed tiger flickered back. "One on top of the other..."

"Are they as old as they look, Professor?" the younger man asked her. He seemed excited, like the dancers who waved their spears.

71

"These have been here twenty thousand years, Tony. At least."

The young man began to laugh. "Bingo!" he said.

"Don't talk like that," the woman replied. "This is a sacred place."

"You don't believe that stuff, do you?" Tom mocked. "These paintings will make our reputations! Yours included!"

"Only if you keep them secret," Tony warned. "Or Jack's lot will get in first. We need a camera crew down here tomorrow."

The leader turned away. His face bore the expression humans call anger, but he said nothing.

Going nearer him, the woman stood looking at the paintings. "I've dreamt all my life of finding somewhere like this," she said. "But now I feel guilty. Even our breath will damage them."

"I told Tom that," he replied. "He wouldn't listen. Too many pound signs."

The other men were talking loudly, fetching baggage up and down and flashing lights onto my sides. Reindeer and bear appeared, then vanished into night, only to appear again. I became weary of their voices. It was time for them to leave but they did not. They made me hot with their lights, and their comings and goings irritated me. They were like the dung flies that swarmed around my entrance.

So I stretched, and let the cooling stream flow through my channels.

Crying out, the woman turned. "The stream's rising," she called. "It must be raining up top."

"Just a shower," Tom replied. "No need to panic. The forecast was dry."

"That stream's definitely rising," Dan said. "We must go." He gathered his baggage.

The other men lingered on the ledge. "I'll just take a few more shots," Tony called.

"There isn't time!" Dan shouted. "I'm going - even if you aren't."

"Wait for me," the woman called. They slithered down together urgently, towards the gap where they had entered.

I let them go. Their lamps flickered as they scrambled over the rocks and into the darkness.

"We need to convince the money men," Tony said, squatting down and pointing some object at my wall. His voice echoed around my vastness, like an insect's buzz. He annoyed me, yet still he lingered, making clicking sounds and flashing lights.

So I stretched again. Water gushed through my veins.

"Come on!" Tom shouted. "Or we'll get trapped!"

They began to panic, sliding down my rocks in a maddened flight. Crying out in pain they fell and scrambled up again. Together they began to wade the stream. It was up to their waists. One fell. He grabbed at the other man, until they both fell. Their lights shone briefly through the water, passing under the roof of the channel. Then they went out.

For a long time I have waited for someone to return. They do not come. In the silence drops fall gently from my roof, with the rhythm of ages. ⁄⁄

73

Greg Freeman

The Corn Mother

Trudging uphill through Surrey shingle,
the seasoned wood is suddenly a beach,
trapped coral and fossils. Cruel-edged flints
litter path; weapon heads, stone walls, the vital spark.

Foxgloves huddle within the coombe. Poppies
teased and rippled on the field margin
flirt and loiter beside the barley,
waiting for a corn mother to step their way ⁄⁄

Rose Drew
Beckon

Chris is dizzy. His mind spins, really spins, like a top: he imagines his pink squishy brain rotating unevenly inside the red bowl of his skull. Oh no, not again. Bracing hands onto knees, he leans over and spills out pints of lager, chunks of white chips, onto to the pavement. Finished, he staggers upright, wipes his mouth with the back of his hand, sags against the brick wall. The world tilts.

What was it he wanted to do...? The night's a blur: Mandy yelling at him, his mates yelling at him, the landlord tossing him out the pub. My change is on the bar! he remembers, shit. Not fair. None of it's fair. First his job, now everyone is angry with him, and his bit of money gone too? Spilled out, he grins. Like chips too cold and thick to start with, and lager.

Chris leans onto the building, then staggers down to the low river wall, where he sits, facing town. Hell with them. He turns toward the glittery river, swings his legs over the tow-path. Ah, that's better. So calm. Distantly he hears music, jangly guitars and loud voices. Thump-thump. Who's that band then, he wonders. Naw, can't tell and he doesn't care. Gazing at the smooth, shiny blackness of the Ouse, slim wavery reflections pulsing, Chris fights to focus on the night, to puzzle out what went so horribly wrong.

Mandy, and she's in her red top with the silvery squiggles along the neckline - the tit line really, so low cut-made me angry, he recalls. Her and Jim, they was leaning on the bar and Jim says something funny and Mandy leans forward to laugh way too long, not that hilarious was it, and her tits spilling out the red glittery neck. Did he... did he hit Jim? Or, Oh no, he groans: did he pop Mandy? Couldn't have done. Not our Mandy. But why is he out here, cold and sick, not with his mates and his money and Mandy? What else...? The river slants, the barrier bobs gently, like a moored boat, Chris closes his eyes and places both hands onto the wall.

"Chris....... Chris......" moans a female voice tenderly, soft like music, like sex, near his ear. Chris pops up his eyelids, arms and neck tingly with the vibration of the voice, so nearby. "Who, what, I can't see you," he mutters, swaying on the wall as he manoeuvres his unfocused gaze to the right, then the left. "Man... Mandy? Is that you, girl?"

"Chris....... Chris....." the voice repeats, trailing damp words across his shoulders, into his neck, causing ripples of raised hairs to spread out from her whispers. He feels someone settle beside him. Chris peers blearily to his right.

"I, I don't see you. Who is it? It ain't you, is it Mandy? Do I know you...?" he finishes miserably, uncertainly. "I don't think I'm good company, if you're looking for someone, not tonight."

"Chris...... Chris...... Come with me. Come now. I want you. Chris...." the voice wheedles sweetly, damply drawing Chris to teeter on rubber legs. He can't even feel the cobbles beneath his trainers; he is so tired...... so tired...... the nausea fades, as exhaustion begins to push him back down.

"No...... Chris..... not there, come with me....... it's warm and friendly.......... Chris.....," the voice urges kindly, repeatedly, lifting him back to swaying, tentative steps. The tow-path slopes gently down to the river, and he's pulled by gravity and the lovely, persuasive woman whispering encouragement. He stumbles; a cold hand meets his chest, halting his fall. "No..... Chris..... walk slowly. Take your time... We have now't but time...... come with me... Come........ come with me, Chris..."

Chris walks, unsteadily, down to the river's edge, down to the cement restraining wall, the corner rough as sandpaper, sharply angled a sudden end to the path. No steps descend to the surface here. Just the embankment, Chris eases onto the cement, dangling his legs over the side. The river doesn't brush his feet; tide's out, he reasons. So nice..... so quiet.... the blaring thumpa-thumpa rock music much fainter. The girl he can't quite see, even by the moonlight, sits near him: he can feel her presence, but not her warmth.

"Who are you?" he finally asks, breaking into the soft lap of the water to the embankment, "and why can't I see you? Am I that drunk?"

"Chris...... you're perfect..... I can see you..... you've had a bad night, your friends have mistreated you...... I can be your friend...... your only friend..... the only one who cares....." she murmurs, soft as water, lapping at his ear, spilling calm chills across his chest, arms, down his legs. "Come, Chris....... No need to be lonely...... no worries...... no loneliness...... come...... come......" The voice grows urgent, insistent, filling his head with words and sounds and the promise of.... of something. Boat? Does she have a barge downriver? Are they near some steps? That water will be cold, Chris reasons ponderously; maybe we shouldn't be this close....

"Chris!" shrieks the voice, hurting his ears as cold damp hands shove his back, other hands grab his shirt, and the voice again, "Chris!" It sounds loud, so loud, and no longer friendly. Chris is falling, briefly, then into the cold wetness. "Oh dammit!" he shouts, "no!" Chris is panicking. Cold! Cold and heavy! Shoes filling with water, trousers weighing him down, those hands, the water..... Blackness closes over him, stinging his eyes, shutting his mouth.... hold his breath, that's what he'll do, get this crazy bitch away from him. Cold. Sleepy. So heavy, everything's heavy, heavy and cold, her voice still filling his ears, his eyes, his mind, his lungs.

She smiles. So easy, these humans. So simple to catch. All it takes is a bad night. ⚄

John Coopey
Yggdrasil

Beneath the roots of the Tree of Life,
The mythical Yggdrasil,
Live the Three Sisters of Fortune,
Three spinners sit weaving still.

Our fortunes favoured, fortunes damned,
Are spun to dusk from dawn,
The destinies of every man
Ordained before we're born.

Spun threads of rope and threads of silk
And threads of finest gold;
With every one a path of life
The Spinners have foretold.

Embittered entertainment prompts
Their play with our distress;
They weft and warp our misery
With transient happiness.

Even the most blessed threads
May still incur their wrath,
Sometimes are spun through deeper roots
To weave a darker cloth.

The rarest threads, the bravest lives
Led so resolutely,
But as with gold debase to dust
Corrupted absolutely.

They spin the hopes we seek fulfilled,
And bring them dashing down
They weave our ways to where they wish
Then laugh beneath the ground.

Life's choices are illusory,
And false we have free will;
Oh cruel Sisters of the Tree!
Oh fickle Yggdrasil! //

Amy Christmas

Kali

She turned up a few minutes late,
after I'd stopped screaming rustic curses at the sky,
and was looking about myself
red-faced and sweating,
at passers-by who stared right back
and avoided coming too close.

"Where were you?" I shouted -
and she just blinked her huge dark eyes
and let a sigh trickle from parted lips.

"Are you sure you want to do this?" she asked me sceptically -
and it struck me strange that she of all people should be
rational.

I thought about it.

And then the anger slipped away as quickly as it came;
ebbing out of me to leave shingle and gasping gills exposed.

"No," I replied -
and I filled up and overflowed,
splashing her jewelled feet with liquid frustration.

She put her four tattooed arms around me
and held me tight until it passed,
and with her long tongue she licked away my tears
in one graceful movement. //

Pauline Kirk

In the Bar, Covent Garden

Ah! You recall me now:
the fat soprano in helmet and horns.
To you I am operatic fun. Strange –
you know foreign ghosts, but not us,
your Viking ancestors.

The Norsemen knew me:
Brunhild, a goddess with power
to choose who would die – and the reward.
True, their heaven would not suit your taste,
all that drinking and slaying...
not my idea of bliss either.

The living were my desire: a warm body
next to mine, strong hands about my waist.
You doubt, seeing this sunken mouth and eyes,
but once my beauty lit a king's hall.

What's that? Immortality grants eternal youth?
Oh that it did! No ...just memory haunting time,
without end. Let me tell you how it really was,
before Wagner stole midnight tales,
and cobbled them to four hours of tedium.

Gunnar - the man who would be wed to me –
was no more a hero than that corseted tenor.
He dared not ride through fire to win me,
and then blamed his horse. How was I to know
he would not dare again, but let his friend
shape-shift into his place, and my love?

Such loving too! Sigurd was mine,
and yet he returned to Gudrun...
So I gave orders. And I am a goddess.

I have grieved an eternity since,
but no one mocks a Valkyrie, even you.
As you gulp your interval drink,
remember this: Death can speak any tongue,
hunt anywhere, even stalk an opera house. //

John Gilham

The Fish-Eyes of the Dead

Oh no, my love,
don't let the spectres engulf us:
let us wade into the mud
by Blackfriars Bridge,
kiss our hands to the Mermaid,
search for Roman sandals
and the fish-eyes of the dead.

Southward the Tabard
and the road to Canterbury.
No jewels on the shrine now;
all the saints have a bare home.
Stay, drink of the river;
we will search for Roman sandals
and the fish-eyes of the dead.

Turn this way, my love.
Don't go uphill to Cheapside,
to Cornhill and Lombard Street,
but sway with me forever
between Greenhithe and Fulham;
we will search for Roman sandals
with the fish-eyes of the dead. ⁄⁄

Jim Fairfoot
Existential Pizza

You order your Quattro Stagioni from the Existential Pizza
Service, because it sounded interesting, and you thought it
might be unusual, a bit out of the ordinary, above average.
You make a tea - milk, one sugar - and wait. Doorbell. You
open the door. Not exactly familiar, but there's something
about him like me. You can't get it out of your head, but it's
a pizza delivery man, so it can't be me, can it? Five. Not the
cheapest, but let's see what it amounts to. He hands you the
box.

"That's a bit light." Your two hands, expecting a certain
weight, rise up. There's hardly anything to it.

"Feel free to check the contents. We like you to get what
you ordered."

You turn one edge out of the cardboard slots and open the
box. It's empty.

"But there's nothing in it."

"Ah, that depends on your perception. It's a pizza box, so
that implies it contains a pizza."

"But here's nothing in it."

"You ordered a Quattro Stagioni. It's written in the
category space on the box top."

And so it is. And the box is warm, quite hot, in fact - too
hot to hold for long.

"I'd better put this down."

You go inside and put the box on the plate you had ready,
on the table by the tea. You'd even warmed the plate - pizza
dough can get cold quickly, even when it's cooked and
straight from the oven, and this had travelled. Wait a
minute. There's nothing in there. You go back to the door.

"There's nothing in it."

"Look - the box is a pizza box. That's at least fifty per cent
of the evidence. The label tells you what's in it. That's even

more persuasive. In what other circumstances do you get so much evidence of reality?" His eyes look upwards and he shakes his head in a sort of resigned way. He's had to deal with this difficulty so often. "Look, you need to show more trust, more belief. Reality, if you want to call it that, doesn't always function by your rules, your perceptions of the moment. You need to trust me."

And you look at him, and again it seems to look like me, but it can't be. It's a pizza delivery man. You're shocked at the sheer effrontery, but somehow you can't resist the logic. You turn to one side and fumble in your purse. Five. You actually give him five. He smiles, and again he seems to look like me.

"Enjoy," he says, and tips an imaginary hat. Then he turns and goes down the stairs.

You shut the door and go back in, and then you have to go to the window, just to see the van. You look out. There's just a seat, at the side of the road. He looks just like me, and he sits down. His feet move, but there are no foot pedals. His hand moves where there ought to be a gear stick, and then he holds both hands out to a steering wheel that just isn't there. But then the seat, with him on it, suddenly moves off at a fair speed, accelerates down the road, round the corner, and he's gone.

You turn back and walk to the table. You look at the plate. There's a pizza on it. ⁂

John Walford
Fear

I am not superstitious.
I am down to earth,
non spiritual
and take a logical, hard nosed
approach to things.

Unsurprising then,
that i have never encountered
a ghost -
and nor am i likely to.
It is not just the fact
that i have no fear of ghosts;
more a case that *they*
are afraid of *me.* ⚏

Joan Keiter

A Trio of You
Poems for the Ghost in My Bed

I Believe I Remember

I can't remember anything after I kissed you.

I don't remember you
But, I remember you in me.

You see.
I save everything.
I'm a collector.
I know the human race.
I have rubbed them all over my body and yelled at them when
they didn't agree with me.
Of course they knew I knew you before I was born.
In a meadow.
By a hemlock.

And then, with the years torn away like pages in a calendar,
carved by ghosts on my tomb.

I was hidden under the floorboards and creaked over for years
until you mentioned my name and I turned and fell and cried.

That's what of remember of love.

It Was Then

I've made love seven times today;
To the door,
To the past
And my ghosts and their cousins
Satin children all lined up ready to see me fail.
I drank a cup of tea in the room labelled loneliness
And then cracked my vein open and fed it drugs from the
graveyard

Ones I had collected that morning, distilled from frost and
suffering with empathy.
It was then that I caught myself in the mirror
Propped up at the tomb of myself in the future.
I was playing at the cinema.
My head was the projector and my eyes saw what you will
never see.
Your contempt for me, which you keep hidden in a little canvas
satchel, under the bones that used to be our bed.

The Epilogue

Which part of the book did you read?
I started at the epilogue; the scene with you lowering my ghost
into her crimson grave, filled with torn kisses and magnets that
attract the unknown.

Your second wife hurling a flower, only be caught by your third.
The children circling like dogs round a pit.
We all lived our life as if there was only one of us.

Now I parade round your memories, like their keeper, dressed
in a shroud sewn from reminders of what I was when your dead
song filled the air.

What love was that, splattered upon the alter, thrown upon the
tomb?
I will walk through your interior for years to come.
Bumping into him and her and all of them that you were with
when you weren't with me.
Devil child you used to call me when I spat blood at your letters
from the dead.
Your bones clutch my flesh from the insides,
Your whispers call from half way down the cliff.

Who am I when you don't want me? //

Val Horner

August

The heat of summer held us in thrall;
gardens shrivelled, a lingering smell of
cat and privet; bone-white lanes wearied through
parched land, yellow with chaff and drying dung,
the sky loured, a sour milky blue.

Limbs felt heavy, slow to respond,
tomorrow receding, into the past,
yesterday's expectations left to fade,
as streams whispered to a trickle, ponds
shrank and the sea drifted a dream away.

I climbed up to the shade of the high wood,
where a hawk combed the valley below,
bruised clouds, building to the south, and
a shock of wind rattled the leaves, sending
a pigeon clattering from its bough,

as a bolt of light ripped the scene asunder,
and the rains came, flattening the grass.
Love, I saw you. Your long, thin, black shadow
racing across the fields, your green hair
flowing, your arms laden with flowers. //

Clint Wastling
Moon's Child

When you buy the house you've always dreamed of I suppose you can't expect everything to go smoothly. Firstly the bed wouldn't go upstairs and finally despite all efforts to push it through the patio doors, the sofa ended up in the garage and not the lounge. Becky and I sat cross-legged on the floor, an empty lager can standing between us.

We tried smiling at each other but the day had been exhausting. Becky leant against me and sighed. I put my arm round her and looked around the room. Without a carpet and sofa, and piled with boxes at precipitous angles, the room still retained the presence which made us both tumble out of the place after our first viewing and say simultaneously, "That's the one!" We laughed, then realised the vendor might be listening and calmed ourselves.

"I'm done in," Becky said.

"I'll lock up." As the bed frame was leaning against the garage wall, we were in separate rooms. Becky had won the toss and got the lilac room, I would be sleeping in Mr. Moon's old room.

Mr. Moon had lived in the house all his life. He was a fey old man; sprightly despite the pipe he took each evening as he sat by the bedroom window and looked down towards the river. Even now Becky found the smell overpowering, hence her preference for the smaller room. There was something curious about it. The walls either side of the door didn't match. One was a thin studded wall, the other thick stone.

Despite my overwhelming tiredness I was still excited at being in the house of our dreams. Moonlight streaming through the window reminded me of many happy nights as a child. I stood up in my sleeping bag and waddled towards the leaded lights. For a moment I caught a glimpse of my face in the glass, the twilight made me look drawn. I ignored this and looked out on the vista rendered in shades of silver and grey. The lawn contained by its overgrown hedges gave way to meadows that were severed by the meandering river. A bat cut swathes though the air and from somewhere underneath the full moon came the sound of a musician, a merry tune was taken up on a fiddle. I listened intently. I wished my own recorder were unpacked so I could play along. I lost track of time.

At dawn I found myself lying on the mattress listening to the window creak on its hinges as bird song emptied into daylight.

"What an awful night!" Becky said as she flumped downstairs." I hardly slept at all. Do you know the floor isn't level? I felt as though I were in a boat! And to cap it all I was sick as soon as I got up."

"Sick again? Nerves. They say moving house is really the most stressful thing you can do. Still look at the wonderful opportunity of owning a four hundred year old uneven floor!" I joked.

Becky slammed cupboard doors and drawers. "Where's the coffee?"

"Here!" I said and ladled a spoonful into each cup.

"I told you -- never buy a house just because you fall in love with it! That's no way to make money."

"I wasn't thinking of the building as an investment, more of a home, somewhere for us to be happy."

"There you go being impractical again!" Becky pushed the coffee away. "On second thoughts I'll have water. That smells awful!"

. "We ought to think of a name for the place." I suggested.

"I think 11 Riverview is good enough."

"You used to have imagination, Becky. Look I can see all this is getting you down. Let's take an hour off and grab a sandwich in the local?" To my relief she agreed.

On the way back I noticed how our cottage stood back from the road with lupins and hollyhocks striding down the border. Becky's arm reached round me. "Sorry I've been so grotty. I needed the break and it was nice to meet folk. Fancy them calling it Moon's Cottage."

"We should have a name plaque made." I ventured.

"We've got more important things to spend our money on." Becky kissed me on the cheek as we walked over the threshold.

All afternoon we worked in separate rooms until there was some order in the lounge, minus its sofa, the kitchen and bathroom. I walked around the garden and then opened up the shed. It smelt of damp and paraffin. Cobwebs festooned the windows and beams. The structure was empty apart from one item, a dull oblong of metal. I polished it with my sleeve. It was a name plaque. "Moon's Cottage." I ran back to the house and got my tools. Becky followed me to he front door and tutted disapprovingly. A few minutes later the cottage had regained its name. I felt happy.

Before retiring that night I propped Becky's bed level. She thanked me and fell into a deep sleep; one arm around me and her long auburn hair covering my shoulder. I longed to stay but Becky looked so peaceful I couldn't disturb her.

I tiptoed to my room and readied myself for bed. I looked through the window. I was reminded of a picture which hung in my childhood bedroom and decided to seek it out amongst the boxes. It was almost as though it wanted to be found and when I stood at the window, I could almost feel my father's arm comfort me. The smell of tobacco brought me back to reality. Its flavour was fresh. Mr. Moon might only just have left the room to collect a nightcap.

Sleep eluded me and then the tune began, only this time on a recorder.

"Dad. Dad!" A girl entered the room. Her eyes searched mine. "You're not my dad." She said anxiously and put the instrument down on the windowsill. Her body dissolved into the wall leaving only the echo of that melody. When I looked there was no trace of the recorder but the tune was answered by music from across the river. I searched the house in panic but found no evidence of an intruder. I lent out of the window and lit a cigarette. I looked at the stars then flicked my cigarette into the unknown. An owl screeched. I closed the window and lay down on the bed.

"It's amazing what a good night's sleep can do. I've been up an hour already and got the sideboard organised. Your recorder's in the left hand drawer." She flicked the curled piece on card onto the table. It left a trail of dust.

"It's an old photo."

I flattened the black and white image of a man and young girl. I felt my throat tighten.

"What is it?" Becky asked.

"The girl. I saw her last night. She came into my room..."

"You're over tired."

I accepted Becky's assertion but looking at the picture again I was certain this was the girl I'd seen as she proudly clutched a recorder.

I took my own out of the drawer and played the tune I'd heard.

"I think the room with the view should be ours. I'd enjoy looking out of the window before going to sleep...

"That's where you went last night! I know it's smaller but the lilac room is warmer, friendlier... and it doesn't smell of stale tobacco."

"I find it quite reassuring. The stale tobacco smell is me." I added guiltily.

"You worry me." Becky said. "Sometimes I think you've become different since we moved."

"I've got an idea. We could knock down the dividing wall and make one big room on that side of the house. There are still the two others as spares for guests."

"And any little extras."

There was something in the way Becky said the line which made me suspect. "Are you pregnant?" I asked.

Becky nodded, smiled and broke into tears and I found I was laughing and crying at the same time.

91

The knock at the door was an unwelcome intrusion. A uniformed police woman stood admiring the flowers. "Sorry to disturb you, it's a long shot but have you seen Mr. Moon?"

"No, why?"

"He left the care home this afternoon in an agitated state. Said he was going to stay with his daughter."

"No, sorry, we can't help."

"Well, if you do see him please give me a ring." She held out a card and I took it.

"He must be very sad." Becky said closing the door. "What's wrong?" Her intuition came to the fore.

"It's silly but do you ever hear music?"

"That's the great thing about the place. The silence to pour your thoughts into..."

"Yes." I lied.

That night, a full moon, the landscape came to life once more. I opened the window and tried to play the tune the minstrel performed. I couldn't get it right. The breeze carried the notes I attempted. They were answered by a fiddle.

"I'd love to play that tune." I said.

"Come and join me and you will" was the reply. I looked around the room. It wasn't Becky playing a joke. The musician's notes wove around me and intrigued I went downstairs with my recorder.

One moment I was walking across the lawn, the next I was dancing over the meadow.

"Play a tune," the little girl said with a smile, "we'll make a merry band."

I began to play. At first the notes emerged staccato but slowly they achieved a form until the tune became a melody.

We played and danced along the lane, through the meadow and down to the river. My companion dissolved into the night and I realised I couldn't stop playing. I tried to throw the recorder away but my fingers were stuck to the surface;

the mouthpiece remained fixed to my lips. I struggled and panicked but still the tune went on. The notes called a boat. A solitary oarsman heaved away. The rower jumped out and pulled the boat up onto the shore.

"Good evening." said Mr. Moon. He placed a pipe between his lips

Try as I might I couldn't stop playing, on and on it went. My fingers felt tired and sore but still I played on. I looked up at the windows of Moon's Cottage. Becky waved frantically. As soon as Mr. Moon sat me in the boat I thought I was lost. I thought of all those precious moments with Becky, touching her auburn hair, feeling her slender body beneath my arms, listening to her breathe: in, out, in out. The boat was cast adrift and I heard water move beneath the oars. Mr. Moon put down his pipe, folded a letter and placed it in my shirt pocket. Finally he picked up the violin and played melancholic music.

"You really do love her." he said.

Becky was running down toward the bank. "Don't leave me. Don't leave us!" She shouted. The moon sank beneath a cloud.

Still my fingers danced over the notes.

"Us?" Mr. Moon smiled. "The patter of tiny feet in my cottage again? Play a tune for her when she's born." He said.

The recorder fell from my lips.

"Play my tune for your daughter."

That's when I saw he was crying as though some long ago event weighed heavily upon him.

"Your daughter?" I asked.

He nodded, "Treat her gently when you find her." He rowed back to the bank.

"David! I love you!" Becky had waded into the river and was waving hysterically. Her voice beseeched and I jumped out to catch her in my arms. She kissed me then turned me round and pointed. Mr. Moon and his daughter were drifting out into the river laughing and playing a merry tune.

"I thought you were bewitched." She said.

"I think I was, or so tired I couldn't tell."

"Read this." I said when we'd got back to the cottage and dried.

"That's sad, so sad." Becky said and let the paper fall.

I picked it up and scanned the page. It all made sense. Mr. Moon couldn't bear to part with his daughter even in death. He had buried her here and hidden her belongings in the wall of her room.

"Come in," I said on hearing the knock.

"Sorry to disturb you again only I thought you should hear officially, news travels fast in a small village. Mr. Moon took a rowing boat onto the river. I'm sorry to say we've found his body."

I passed over the letter.

Nobody spoke and from the silence I heard the tune, first on the recorder, then the violin rallied in support. "Do you hear that?" I whispered and I could see from the look on their faces that everyone did. ⁄⁄

Jane Wilcock

The West Window
A Saga of York and Constantine 306

The Christmas markets squeeze the cobbled streets,
Rain pours cold upon the mulled wine shoppers,
Colours in the dark, shiny bags of presents,
Stalls of chocolates, pastries, sausages, olives –
Olives from Italy, all colours, sizes, marinades,
And in that black afternoon of gift shopping they came –
The Italians.

We heard their marching feet upon the stone first,
Saw the flaming torches abreast their tunics,
Watched the ancient Roman legions process,
Past stalls, boutiques, eateries, the bustling shoppers:
We stepped back.

Their red plumes dripped onto helmeted features,
Rain ran down gold studded leather,
Drenching the marching feet of strong fighting men.
Behind, wheels clacked and hooves slipped
Where two white stallions slowly pulled a bier,
And at the last a young man rode,
His face a mask of grief, tears running with the rain:
Upright upon his black horse.

Constantine, heir to Constantius,
Whose body lay stiff as ice upon the bier,
Proclaimed Augustus to the Western Empire,
Paraded his father to the populous,
In York.

Through Swinegate and round the streets to the River Ouse
Where the funeral pyre lay ready to launch and burn.
Mars and Venus, the Gods of War and Love, formed above them
And we shrank back with our bright bobble hats and scarves,
And watched them pass: half fear, half wonder,
Then they stopped.

Silently the Legions stood before Gothic arches and towered spires,
An unexpected obstruction to their passage.
Constantine rode forward, glancing at seated statue of himself
And urged his horse upon the steps
And to the Minster.

Through the great doors and down the nave,
He wheeled his horse back to the Quire and altar,
Inspecting the church as he would inspect his men, he smiled:
His first for weeks.

Here stands the birth of a Christian Empire,
Years of politics, debate, persecution, favours,
The Roman Emperor saw through the centuries,
Heard the carols upon the organ, saw the love upon the altar,
St Peter within the walls and pillars.
The real birth had not been easy either;
Though it was simple.

Outside, we, with our shopping, watched them flicker and fade
Like a dream from the past the space filled with air,
We thanked God for Christ and the people
Who have witnessed, believed
That faith runs through York's veins like the Minster the
years. //

Adrian Spendlow

Bathhouse of Blood

Noises and movement   I hear often   and if I awake to them
in hours so early   As I step from the stairs   I am among
them   Crushing it is   Their bulk pressing into me   and the
fear   the anticipation   is vastly apparent   Here, in this,
early hours slaughter house   that now is my home   the
spirits of many   beast-like remain   still trapped in
recollection   that this is the morning   Huddled
together here   these memories of cattle are
awaiting the doorway   that leads to their slaughter

Far better to experience this   than the lot of my neighbour
he sleeps in his basement room   and wakes on a morning
to a feeling of wetness   slapping down on his face
suddenly awakened to   a feeling most sickly   a
clamminess covers him   and clings to a memory
he thinks this is quirky   soon shrugs off the feeling   I
cannot let myself tell him   of the spirit-husk livestock
which are led from my lounge here   through a ghost
door to above him   and a timelessness death cut   pouring
their lifeblood   through a ginnel-run downwards   to
awake him so rudely   to bathe him each morning   in a
terrible haunting   of the blood and the gore //

Robin Lewis
Sidelined

what they are is no longer mainstream
　　what they do is no longer acceptable

it is apparently cookoo.

　　　what they believe is no longer true
　　　(though what any of us believe has never been true

　　　　and theirs is as good a lie as any)

　　　the things they do and the things they are
　　　are no longer considered right, but that will change

　　　as it has always changed and it will change when they become
mainstream again and

I look forward to those days. ⁄⁄

Biographies

Amina Alyal
is a poet and a lecturer in English literature. Her interests cover Renaissance literature, poetry, drama, oratory and myth. She is based at Leeds Trinity University College, and has published academic articles and original poetry. She has written for music and musical performance and is currently working on two collections of poetry, provisionally entitled *Seasons of Myth* and *The Ordinariness of Parrots.*

Malin Bergström
has always been the one to take the awkward route. One might say that this makes her life infinitely more interesting. Or one might claim that she's flaky and un-predictable. But really, she's something of a social traveller: the eternal warrior following the route of the sun, keeping the rays to heat up the night. Dawn is her favourite time of day where she relies on the cross-roads to show her the truth. And when she can't decide where to go she writes poetry amongst other things.

Andrew Brown
is a performer of a great many characters and voices. He has read his stories and poems across Yorkshire and regularly broadcasts his material on Tempo FM. He is co-author of a book of Harrogate-related ghost stories called *Stray Ghosts* (2008) and his CD of short stories, *Andy in Short Shorts*, appeared in 2010. He also has stories in the Stairwell railway anthology *Along the Iron Veins.*

Helen Burke
has been writing poetry for 40 years and performing it for 30. She writes comedy sketches and plays and is a regular reader on East Leeds FM Radio. Recently she read in Paris at the American Library; and later in the year will read in the Loire Valley and in Romania. Recent collections include *The Ruby Slippers* the very new *And God Said Let There be Chocolate*. She is published in the U.S. Her work is widely anthologised and appears in many magazines including *Rialto, New Welsh Review, Oxford Magazine, Raindog,*

IMPPress, Domestic Cherry, the French Literary Review and others.

Amy Christmas
is careering towards the end of her PhD in Literature at York St John. Her creative work has been published regularly since 2006 in the UK and the USA.

David Cooke
won a Gregory Award in 1977 and published *Brueghel's Dancers* in 1984. His retrospective collection, *In the Distance*, was published in 2011 by Night Publishing. A new collection, *Work Horses*, will be forthcoming in 2012 from Ward Wood Publishing. His poems and reviews have been accepted widely in journals such as *Agenda, Ambit, The Bow Wow Shop, Critical Quarterly, The Frogmore Papers, The Irish Press, The London Magazine, Magma, New Walk, The North, Orbis, Poetry Ireland Review, Poetry London, Poetry Salzburg Review, The Reader, The SHOp, Stand* and *Tears in the Fence.*

Ed Cooke
plays bass and writes lyrics for UK rock band Voyager Project. He has written half-a-dozen stage musicals and one short film.

John Coopey
The essence of poetry for John is performance and rhythm. He writes on various subjects from history, rail travel, work and play. His main talent, though, is making people laugh. He has been published in *Along the Iron Veins, Pen 10 Compendium* and *Aquillrelle: Anthology 1.* An accomplished guest poet available for weddings, funerals and bar mitzvahs!

J.E. Cremins
Jo Elizabeth Cremins is an English lecturer and a writer. Her stagework has been performed as part of the New Writing Festival at Harrogate Theatre and in the one-minute transatlantic show *Gi60.* She has a special interest in Yorkshire dialect and has extensively researched local language for museum collections. She continues to be fascinated as to how dialect can be used to tell stories, both of people and places.

Rose Drew
wants to believe in an Afterlife, when she can spy on the
living, cackle and mutter things like "You're wearing
THAT?" In 15 years of sorting skeletons, even at 3 am, Rose
has yet to hear voices or see items moving by themselves,
although she often feels watched. But there was that time
the drinking cup flew sideways...

Rose is addicted to hosting open mics, having run one
somewhere in the world for over 9 years. Her poetry and
prose has appeared in newspapers, magazines, online
venues; and books including *100 Days*, *The Machineries of
Love*, *Wednesdays at Curley's*, and *Crush*. Her book,
Temporary Safety, Fighting Cock Press, was No 9 on the
Purple Patch 2011 20 Best Individual Collections.

Tim Ellis
does not believe in ghosts, nor that choirboys transmute into
birds. He was not a collector of animal skeletons and has
never known anybody named Keith Fowler. He is however a
keen bird watcher, amateur naturalist, world-traveller and
poet, and at some time in the 1970s he was indeed a member
of the St. Michael and All Angels' Church Choir, in a village
in Berkshire. Occasionally he includes a little bit of truth in
his poems, a collection of which was published by Stairwell
Books under the title *Gringo on the Chickenbus*. 2011 was a
good year for Tim: he won 1st prize in the Huddersfield
Grist Poetry Competition, and was crowned York Poetry
Slam Champion.

Jim Fairfoot
writes and performs poetry and stories, and has a novel
under submission to a London agent. His poetry is
published in the late summer edition of *Orbis*, and slated for
publication in the next issue of *Dream Catcher*. He has
lectured in Creative Writing in Medical Humanities at the
University of Leeds, is a Visiting Lecturer in Life Writing on
the University of Teesside's MA Creative & Professional
Writing, but has his principle commitment as an Associate
Senior Lecturer in Writing Practices at Leeds Trinity
University College. He holds a Leeds University MA
Distinction in Creative Writing.

Greg Freeman
works as a newspaper sub-editor, and is also news editor for
the poetry website Write Out Loud. He came to York to
follow his love and flee from the south in the last century,
and retains many happy memories of the city, particularly
the pubs.

John Gilham
Fosdyke and Me and Other Poems is published by Stairwell
Books and Fighting Cock Press. His enthusiasms include
poetry, ferroequinology, pubs and beer, and cycling. He is
often to be heard reading his work at the York open mics,
The Spoken Word and *Speakers' Corner*.

Alan Gillott
with his partner Rose Drew, is co-host of *The Spoken Word*
open mic in York. Publications include poems in *The
Nightcap Book*, Blue Dragon Press, and *Community of Poets*
Issue 20, the Connecticut Poetry Society's *Long River Run*,
Turn of the River Press' *Wednesdays at Curley's* and the
University of Toledo's *Poems for Peace*. Alan has featured in
both England and the United States.

Oz Hardwick
is a York-based writer, photographer and musician, whose
most recent poetry collection, *The Illuminated Dreamer*
(Oversteps, 2010), has led to readings from Glastonbury
Festival to the United States, via countless back rooms of
pubs. A keen collaborator with other artists, he has had
work performed in the UK, Europe, US and Australia. To
pay the mortgage he is programme leader for English and
Writing at Leeds Trinity University College.

Michael Hildred
from Bolton near York, is a practising painter and
performance poet, with a background in art, education and
drama. He lectured in Edinburgh for 20 years and, having
published extensive research into art appreciation for
schools in 1989, he took early retirement to return to his
native Yorkshire in 1991. Over the years his paintings have
featured in many exhibitions and his poems can be found in
numerous anthologies. Three poetry publications have also
chosen his paintings for cover designs. In November 2011,
Stairwell Books published *Late Flowering*, a first book of
poetry combining his poems, pencil illustrations and
artwork.

Val Horner
Born in Portsmouth, later lived in London, Wotton-under-Edge and Harrogate, but considers York, on the banks of the Foss to be home. She has a family; is now retired, but in the past has lectured in Philosophy and Literature.

Andy Humphrey
A.J. (Andy) Humphrey is a freelance writer, part-time law student, trade union activist and former research scientist. His short stories have appeared in *Dark Tales, Scribble and Words*, and in the anthologies *Making Changes* (Bridge House), *Old Magic in a New Age* (Earlyworks Press) and *Spooked* (Bridge House). He has had nearly 50 poems published. His writing has won numerous awards including six First Prizes in national and international poetry competitions, and he was the winner of the Open Short Story category in the 2010 National Association of Writers' Groups' Creative Writing Awards. He spends much of his time promoting up-and-coming writers as a competition judge, workshop leader, and MC of The Speakers' Corner open mic night in York. His writing is heavily influenced by his favourite things which include twilight, fairy stories, English and Celtic folk music, single malt whisky, and Dragons.

Martin Huxter
was born in Great Wakering, Essex in 1960. After living for seventeen years in Vienna, Austria, now lives and works as a painter and poet in Alne, North Yorkshire. He took part in many poetry readings and performances at events and festivals throughout Austria. In 2006 *Perfect Blue Dolphin* was included in the anthology *Vienna Views*, published by Luftschacht. He read the poem in public at the Vienna Lit Festival while sitting on a Viennese style toilet and in 2007 *Last Glimpse of Kim Shine* won second prize in the *People and Places* poetry competition, organized by *Aesthetica Magazine* and Vienna Lit.

Joan Keiter
is a writer, comic and visual artist who has been transplanted from New York to Old York. She has written many poems and has three yet published under her belt. Most famous as a comic in the New York circuit, her one woman show, *Hell, Horses and Women* was sold out every

night to critical acclaim. Joan is presently writing and illustrating a book, *Hush*, which is set in York.

Pauline Kirk
lives in York, and is the author of three novels, *Waters of Time, The Keepers* and *Foul Play*, the last written as PJ Quinn. Ten collections of her poetry have been published. Her poems, stories and articles have been included in many anthologies, and broadcast on local radio. She is Editor of Fighting Cock Press and has appeared at venues and festivals throughout the North.

Robin Lewis
has been a writer since he was at school and his teacher pointed him in the direction of The Love Song of J. Alfred Prufrock. Since then, he has been trying to produce something like that in his poetry, and since he discovered Orwell's *1984*, trying to produce something like that in his prose. He lives in York, he is in his mid-30s and you can read some of his more recent poetry at *A Convenient Place To Start*. He's been making his girlfriend very happy in recent days by putting together a collection of stories about teddy bears.

Steve Nash
is a terrifying creature often found lurking in the lecture theatres of York St John University where he teaches whilst completing his PhD. When not piercing young necks with his ample fangs he serves as the poetry editor for both *Open Wide Magazine* and *Indigo Rising UK*. His poetry has been published widely (usually in blood), and he is featured in the *Grist Anthology of the best poetry of 2012*. If you should ever meet him in a dark alleyway we strongly suggest you run the other way.

Tanya Nightingale
Tanya grew up on the border of three counties (Lincoln, Nottinghamshire and Leicestershire) but counts York as her true home since arriving in 1997. Since then she has been performing her work at various venues around the city. Her poems have been published in magazines including *Poetry Nottingham, Other Poetry* and *Dream Catcher*, for which she is also a regular reviewer. She won the Yorkshire Open Poetry Competition (2008) and was shortlisted in the Malton Poetry Competition (2010) and the Speakeasy Poetry Competition (2011). Her poetry has been part of York

International Women's Week and featured in a two-woman show *She's the Cultured One* with Rose Drew, performed at the Edinburgh Festival Fringe and Malton Literature Festival in 2011. Tanya's other great love is the theatre; in her student days she directed the premiere of *Faust the Musical* which also transferred to Edinburgh.

Dick Ockelton
was born and raised in Grimsby, Lincolnshire. He has lived in Yorkshire for 35 years. A graduate of Reading University, he has had a long and varied career in industry and the public sector. He currently leads on Sustainability and Climate Change for the NHS in Yorkshire and the Humber. In addition to writing, his interests include choral singing, blues music, and walking. He is married with three sons and five grandsons. He is new to the world of published material although he has written for many years. The majority of his work in the past has been for family, friends, and work colleagues, and his output for a wider public has been limited - an imbalance which he is currently attempting to address.

Adrienne Odasso
Adrienne J. Odasso's poetry has appeared in a wide variety of strange and wonderful publications, including *Sybil's Garage, Mythic Delirium, Jabberwocky, Cabinet des Fées, Midnight Echo, Not One of Us, Dreams & Nightmares, Goblin Fruit, Strange Horizons,Stone Telling,* and *The Moment of Change* anthology as well as in several previous Stairwell volumes, *The Exhibitionists, The Green Man Awakes,* and *frisson.* Her short fiction has also appeared both online and in print. Her two chapbooks, *Devil's Road Down* and *Wanderlust,* are available from Maverick Duck Press. Her first full collection, *Lost Books,* was released by Flipped Eye Publishing in April 2010.

PJ Quinn
is the pen name of mother and daughter crime writers Pauline Kirk and Jo Summers. Pauline is a published poet and novelist living in York. Jo lives in Surrey and writes on legal affairs. Their first novel, *Foul Play* (Stairwell Books 2011), is set in the 50's and features Detective Inspector Ambrose. The series continues with *Poison Pen* (late 2012), and *Close Disharmony.*

Helen Sant
Helen M Sant, an occasional poet, has previously published short stories, which include the slightly otherworldly *Storyteller's Tale, (2004)* as part of the *York Tales and three children's tales (2005)* for the Breadcrumbs Trail. She is also a storyteller, in the true oral tradition, specialising in legends and folklore, and sometimes ghost events. Many people have shared their ghostly tales with her over the years. More about Helen's work can be found at www.yorkstoryteller.co.uk.

Adrian Spendlow
Adrian's interest in ghosts comes from his Mum who started ghost walks in the ancient City of York. She introduced him to spiritualism adding contrast to the mix and also gave him the bug for writing and performance. He enjoyed creating this flowing piece in the anthology as an experiment, aiming for an easy style and a spooky engagement.

Paul Sutherland
a Canadian-British poet/writer arrived in the UK in 1973. He has seven collections and has edited seven others. He's the founding editor of *Dream Catcher* a distinguished national-international journal in its 25th issue. He runs creative writing workshops for all abilities and is a frequent public performer of his poetry. His work has appeared in anthologies and journals. Recently he's had a pamphlet *Spires and Minarets* published by Sunk Island Publishing. A new full collection *Journeying* is planned for 2012 from Valley Press. He won the 2008 Nassau Review (US) Poetry Prize for best poem submitted to the journal, came 2nd in the English Association Poetry Prize 2009 and was highly commended in Aesthetica Creative Works Competition the same year. A poem of his has been selected for the Olympics 2012. He turned freelance in 2004.

Andrew Turnbull
is exploring poetry now his children are grown and there is time for other pursuits. He was born in York, and now lives there after living in quite a few other places.

John Walford
was born during a blizzard in Hull in 1947 but has almost recovered. He started writing prose pieces seven years ago and has one published collection entitled *Running with Butterflies* and is currently working on the second.

Clint Wastling
is a writer based in the East Riding of Yorkshire. He's had stories published in "The Weekly News" and online at www.everydayfiction.com. He has a long association with York Writers. His short story anthology, *Calico Blue & Other Stories,* is available in print and Kindle versions.

Jane Wilcock
is a poet based in Bolton. A member of Write Out Loud she has been published in *Mental Virus, Impress ezine,* exhibited at *Wherefore Art Thou?* exhibition at Stockport Art Gallery and *NWNX* exhibition at Wigan, written and directed the children's performance poetry show *Our Little Green Book of Children's Verse* at Edinburgh Fringe and Buxton Fringe. She particularly likes imaginative travels, children's nonsense rhyme and historical sagas.

Gabrielle de Yorvick
was born in Clontarf, Eire and educated in York. She has the typical Celt love of telling stories, reciting poems, and singing folksongs. She wrote her first poem on her 5th birthday and has been writing poetry and short stories ever since. She has just completed her first Children's Book which she is hoping to publish, and is still working on the novel she began two years ago.

Other publications available from Stairwell Books

First Tuesday in Wilton	Ed. Rose Drew and Alan Gillott
The Exhibitionists	Ed. Rose Drew and Alan Gillott
The Green Man Awakes	Ed. Rose Drew
Carol's Christmas	N.E. David
Fosdyke and Me and Other Poems	John Gillham
frisson	Ed. Alan Gillott
Feria	N.E. David
Along the Iron Veins	Ed. Alan Gillott and Rose Drew
A Day At the Races	N.E. David
Gringo On the Chickenbus	Tim Ellis
Running With Butterflies	John Walford
Foul Play	P. J. Quinn
Late Flowering	Michael Hildred
Scenes from the Seedy Underbelly of Suburbia	Jackie Simmons

For further information please contact rose@stairwellbooks.com

www.stairwellbooks.co.uk